PREACHING
THE
REVISED
COMMON
LECTIONARY

GAIL R. O'DAY
CHARLES D. HACKETT

PREACHING THE REVISED COMMON LECTIONARY

A GUIDE

ABINGDON PRESS
Nashville

PREACHING THE REVISED COMMON LECTIONARY
A GUIDE

Copyright © 2007 by Abingdon Press

All rights reserved.

This book is printed on acid-free paper.

Library of Congress Cataloging-in-Publication Data

Hackett, Charles D.
  Preaching the Revised common lectionary : a guide / Charles D. Hackett and Gail R. O'Day.
      p. cm.
  ISBN 978-0-687-64624-1 (binding: pbk., adhesive perfect : alk. paper)
  1. Lectionary preaching.   2. Common lectionary (1992)   I. O'Day, Gail R., 1954– II. Title.

BV4235.L43H33   2007
251'.6—dc22

2007016270

All scripture quotations, unless noted otherwise, are taken from the New Revised Standard Version of the Bible, copyright 1989, Division of Christian Education of the National Council of the Churches of Christ in the United States of America. Used by permission. All rights reserved.

Excerpts from Psalms used in lectionary charts are taken from *The Book of Common Prayer* of the Episcopal Church, 1979.

07 08 09 10 11 12 13 14 15 16—10 9 8 7 6 5 4 3 2 1

MANUFACTURED IN THE UNITED STATES OF AMERICA

To our teachers and our students, from whom we continue to learn.

To John Ruef, who showed Charles Hackett how to be a priest and a critical scholar.

To Paul D. Frazier, ever faithful pastor and preacher.

CONTENTS

PREFACE

A s we, the two authors, have talked during the writing of this book, it seemed to us that although we actually disagreed about very little, when we came to read lectionary texts, our points of view were different. As we discussed this, it became clear that these differences were not the result of our distinct fields (New Testament and liturgical history) nor our teaching experience (Both of us have taught homiletics for a good many years). Nor was it in our educations (Both of us hold the bachelor's degree and the doctoral degree from the same universities!). Rather it is, we think, because we are grounded in different theological traditions. Gail R. O'Day comes from a predominantly Reformed background (United Church of Christ), whereas Charles D. Hackett is an Anglican. This difference has produced some rich conversation between us and has led us to understand that rather than being in competition, each tradition has a good deal to offer the other.

With this in mind it seemed good to us to share some of the particular angles of vision in which these different traditions have formed us and informed our understandings of lectionary preaching.

W hen I come to a set of lessons, my initial reading always imagines them as being read at the Eucharist for the particular Sunday or Holy Day to which they are appointed. My imagination automatically envisions a certain "place" in the liturgical year. Is this the next to last Sunday in Ordinary Time (which is the Second Sunday before Advent)? Or perhaps it is the First Sunday after Epiphany (a traditional time for baptisms). Or perhaps it is the First Sunday of Lent. That is to say, I read these lessons with a sense of location in liturgical time. Where have we just been and where are we headed in this year's pilgrimage through the church year? Part of my imagination is a quite palpable sense of the aura of the day: the liturgical colors, the church decorations, the music's tone and texts, and all the rest, which will be part of that particular day in the liturgical year.

These readings and the sermon that immediately follows them will be part of a community experience in which a group of Christians will come together to become (whether they think of it this way or not) a bit more the holy and loving people of God. In so doing they will listen and look for God, they will seek to pray, and they will relate to each other. They will hear the word read and proclaimed in the context of a certain day or season and will proceed to offer and share the Eucharist.

And so, I find myself aware of the lives of these people in whose midst these readings will be proclaimed. What is happening in the world, in the nation, in the community, in the parish, in their lives? The church year functions to contextualize our lives in terms of the church's experience of our Lord, but it also is meant to open our everyday lives with their pains, anxieties, and joys to the light of the Gospels. What might Luke's account of Jesus' baptism by John (Year C, the First Sunday after Epiphany) mean to a middle Georgia congregation whose only major industry, a textile factory, has just announced it will close its doors? How do fearful events comport with the promises of new life and the healing power of God in Christ that the lessons for this day proclaim?

As I consider this way of beginning to read, which seems by now like second nature to me, it strikes me that it is consistent with the way I understand Scripture. The Bible we have is a combination of Hebrew Scripture (received by the early church primarily in its Greek translation) and those early Christian writings that the church came to define as the "rule" (canon) of the faith. Though there was quite general agreement about the kernel of the New Testament canon by the middle of the second century, the New Testament as we know it was not finalized until the latter part of the fourth century. This nearly miraculous process of consensual agreement took place without the guidance of any central authority and was only ratified by a council in 382 after they had arrived at unanimity. When the church in all its diversity makes a decision like that, even over a period of three and a half centuries, one must attribute it to the Holy Spirit.[1] But the Spirit worked through the church. The Bible as we have it, then, is a product of the thought, the discussion, and, yes, the argument of the church. Perhaps above all, it is linked with the worship of the church, since it was in the gatherings of Christians for

Eucharist and for prayer that the various Gospel accounts, the letters of Paul, and the other writings came to be known. Paul wrote to various churches. He meant for these letters to be read to them assembled. The Gospels almost certainly were intended for public reading at worship, and the argument can be made that any number of portions of New Testament writings were intended for or were parts of such liturgical events as baptismal homilies and instruction. As important as individual reading and pondering and praying with the Bible may be, it always derives from the church's public reading, pondering, and praying. The church year is a primary way of structuring that public engagement, and the *Revised Common Lectionary* is our contemporary attempt at that ancient way of linking worship and Holy Scripture.

But the process of canonizing the Bible was made with constant reference to the experience of Christians. Various, often quite popular, Gnostic writings, for instance, were excluded because they did not represent the earthy and thoroughly physical way that Christians knew they lived. Christ saved precisely because he lived in human flesh and because he suffered and died as each of us suffers and dies. Thus the ancient dictum: "What is not assumed (by Christ) is not redeemed." The Jesus of the Bible is always fully human. So any reading of the Bible that does not acknowledge the full, physical, and mortal humanity of every person is deficient. In this sense, as we come to each Sunday's lessons, we come to an inherited tradition based in the Incarnation of God in Jesus Christ, a tradition that is constantly being formed and reformed by the Church's living experience. We read, we interpret, and we preach in worship to a particular people at a particular liturgical time and a particular time in history. In this biblical reading, worshiping, and preaching, we continually and necessarily modify, if only so slightly, that living tradition that is our Christian inheritance.

And here we come upon another, typically Anglican point of view. Our salvation is rooted in the Incarnation. That means that salvation comes in and through our physical, particular, and historical living. It also means that as we find ourselves in new situations we are bound to discover new ways in which Christ is present and offering life. Christ does not change, but we do. And those changes find him already present in ways and forms unthought by us before.

But these discoveries must be ratified by our brothers and sisters in Christ. None of us alone is free enough from self-centered sin simply to reinterpret the faith by ourselves. Interpretation is ultimately a communal enterprise. As readers and preachers we are called to interpret for our time and our situation, but always with the awareness of our place in the stream of witnesses, past, present and future, which is the church.

Hackett

The liturgical year is not deeply rooted in my imagination in the same way that it is for Charles Hackett. The preached word stood at the center of the worship service in the church in which I was raised and in which I am ordained. For much of my early life, congregations that I attended celebrated the Eucharist ("Communion") monthly, or perhaps quarterly, not weekly, and the liturgical year consisted of marking Christmas Eve, Good Friday, and Easter Sunday. The liturgical rhythms that Professor Hackett notes as the foundation of his pastoral imagination were not a formative part of much of my earliest experience of Christian worship. Instead, the rhythm that formed my pastoral imagination was the exposition of the biblical text. Sunday after Sunday, the sermon was the centerpiece of my worship experience. My sense of worship was that I went to hear the biblical story and to learn what it meant for my life. Reformed traditions have taken as their starting point the Word of God as revealed in Scripture. The biblical texts tell the story of the presence and work of God in and through history, in and through specific communities of faith, and one of the responsibilities of preaching is to create a living conversation between those stories of the past and the present moment of a faith community's life.

In interesting ways, my personal liturgical development reflects the liturgical developments outlined in the opening chapters of this book and that gave rise to the *Revised Common Lectionary*. All of my worship formation occurred after Vatican II and the liturgical renewal that this Council sparked for Protestants and Catholics alike (see chapter 1). In my early adulthood and in the years when I was being formed as a New Testament scholar and homiletician, Protestant churches in the United States went through an amazing liturgical awakening. The sense of the movement of the church year, of the seasons of a worshiping community's life became a regular part of my worship life. The centrality of the sermon in worship did not change, but the context in which that sermon was preached changed dramatically. At first my worship life was only punctuated by a new sense of liturgical time—celebrations of Ash Wednesday, Lent, Advent—but soon my worship life became more regularly shaped by liturgical time. The selection of scripture for worship shared in this new formation. More and more Protestant churches began to use first the *Common Lectionary*, and then the *Revised Common Lectionary*, as the guide in selecting scripture for worship. As a result, my experience of preaching and the role of scripture in worship changed. When the biblical text was read in worship, two stories were now simultaneously in play—the biblical story and the Christian story into which the church year invites the worshiper.

When I read the lectionary texts assigned for a particular Sunday, both of these stories inform my approach. In distinction from Professor Hackett, however, my Reformed orientation and understanding of the centrality of the biblical story lead me to start with the specifics of the biblical text. My initial reading always begins with the lessons as biblical texts and then moves to locate them in the church year. For each of the four lessons provided by the lectionary, I will read the lesson in its entirety and look carefully at its setting in scripture—the biblical book or genre in which it is located (e.g., prophecy, wisdom, narrative, exhortation), the texts which precede and follow it, its contribution and function in the biblical book of which it is a part, its place in the larger biblical story. For me, as someone formed in the Reformed tradition and as a biblical scholar, such questions and investigations are the beginning point of my decision-making about how to appropriate the lectionary texts. The biblical story is the context in which the liturgical story takes place.

I read the liturgical year through the lens of the specific biblical texts assigned for a Sunday or season; Hackett reads the biblical texts through the lens of the liturgical year. I have had to learn, in a way that Hackett did not, what it means to read and worship in the communion of saints through and across time. When the biblical text and the sermon stand at the center of worship, apart from attention to liturgical time, the worship experience is primarily shaped by the content of the sermon—how the preacher uses the biblical text to make sense of the contemporary situation. The lectionary and the liturgical year have helped me experience preaching as more than the exposition of the biblical text and its relevance for today and worshiping as more than a sequence of independent Sundays and sermons. By joining the biblical story with the liturgical year, a preaching ministry can create new ways for a congregation to enter into the story of Jesus' life, death, and resurrection.

Each reader of this book will have his or her own way of achieving the balance and integration of biblical text and liturgical year depending on theological formation and tradition. One of the wonderful gifts of the lectionary to ecumenism (see chapter 4) is that it enables such cross-tradition conversations to take place about something other than doctrine or theological orthodoxy. The lectionary and the engagement of multiple traditions with the liturgical year enable ecumenical conversations about religious practice and spiritual formation, about how we experience the places and times where the Christian story touches our many stories.

O'Day

CHAPTER ONE

AN INTRODUCTION TO CHRISTIAN LECTIONARIES

Lectionaries have been in constant use in many Christian Communions for centuries, and this history of lectionary use is the necessary starting point for understanding the development and use of the *Revised Common Lectionary*. On the broad stage of the church's life and practice, the *Revised Common Lectionary* (RCL) has a history of only about fifty years. Its genesis can be traced to the interest in liturgical renewal in the 1950s and 1960s, but the dominant influences were the liturgical reforms of Vatican II. The Second Vatican Council was determined to use the Sunday Eucharistic celebration as an occasion to, in the words of the Constitution on the Sacred Liturgy, "open up more lavishly" the Bible for those participating in Mass.

This lectionary adapted the ancient pattern of three readings plus a psalm portion. It was designed in a cycle in which the major parts of the Synoptic Gospels would be read successively every three years: Mark in Year A, Matthew in Year B, and Luke in Year C. John was to be read during Advent, Christmas, Lent, and Eastertide. The first or Old Testament reading and the psalm were related to the Gospel of the day, usually on the basis of typology. The second lesson, normatively a portion of an Epistle, was related to the Gospel or the Season in Advent-Christmas and Lent through the Sunday of Pentecost. In the time between Pentecost and Advent ("Ordinary Time"), the Epistles were read on their own without apparent reference to the season.

In North America, the Roman Catholic Church formed a commission to translate and standardize the English texts for the liturgy. In 1965 a number of Protestant and other non-Roman Catholic denominations formed a parallel body, the Consultation on Common Texts (CCT), which eventually included Roman Catholics. This body, in consultation with other ecumenical organizations, was influential in helping several denominations produce the liturgical books and hymnals that are now changing the character of much worship in the United States and Canada. It also produced a version of the Roman Catholic lectionary known as *The Common Lectionary*. This proved popular, particularly as part of the revised liturgies such as those in the United Methodist *Book of Worship* and *United Methodist Hymnal* and the Presbyterian *Worshipbook*. Yet the widespread usage of the *Common Lectionary* also revealed theological and ecclesiological weaknesses, especially with reference to the place of the Old Testament in the lectionary cycles. Some African American denominations, for example, noted the omission of particularly meaningful sections of stories like the Exodus narratives, and some churches in the Reformed traditions wished that the Old Testament could be freed from its consistent typological relationship to the Gospel of the day.

In response, the CCT added longer sections of the Old Testament and various Epistles to be read more or less continuously over several Sundays in Ordinary Time. In addition, readings from the Wisdom literature were added to the Sundays leading to Advent. At the same time efforts were made to enroll English-speaking churches in the United Kingdom, South Africa, New Zealand, and Australia. This resulted in some further modifications leading to the 1992 publication of the *Revised Common Lectionary*.

At the present time, conversations are ongoing with worldwide Protestant bodies and with the Roman Catholic and Orthodox Churches with the hope that eventually all Christians will be reading and hearing the same portions of Holy Scripture on the same Sundays and holy days throughout the world. Given the antiquity of, for instance, the Orthodox lectionaries, this seems a daunting task, but one for which many wish and pray.

Christian Lectionaries: An Overview of Their History

Today, when we hold a copy of the *Revised Common Lectionary* we are holding the result of thousands of years of Jewish and Christian experience. Lectionaries and the rhythm of the liturgical year with which they are bound up have been crucial to the formation of Jewish and Christian souls since at least the Babylonian captivity. The RCL is not simply a systematic way to read the Bible in church services; it has an innate, living dynamic, which was operating in the early church as the very canon of the New Testament was being formed through the church's experience with the Holy Spirit.

To have a sense of that dynamic we must spend some time getting at the history of Christian lectionaries and to do that we must begin with the Jewish synagogue where the first systematic Hebrew lectionaries were born.

The early history of the institution of the synagogue is unclear, but it almost certainly began after Nebudchanezzer systematically deported and dispersed great numbers of Hebrews from Judea in the sixth century B.C.E., with the hopes that they would become absorbed into Babylonian culture. He reasoned that by removing them from their Temple, the center of their worship, and scattering them about a land with foreign language and culture, he could cause them to lose their identity. Counter to these expectations, however, the Judeans found a way to survive. In fact, the foundations for what would become Judaism were laid during the Jewish experience in the Diaspora.

The use of Hebrew Scripture, primarily the Mosaic law found in the Pentateuch, the Prophets, and portions of the Wisdom literature, particularly the psalms, was central to this impressive adaptation. Because these scriptures were systematically read in Hebrew, each Jewish child had to learn the original language of the texts. In the process children acquired knowledge of the common history and hope of their people. In order to facilitate the instruction of children, the synagogue, or "meeting house," evolved as a place for gathering, teaching, and reading. As teachers were needed, the rabbinate developed to instruct students in the Hebrew language and the interpretation of Scripture. Eventually, the Hebrew lectionaries were created as a regularized way to read scripture throughout the year.

The structure of Hebrew lectionaries seems to have been simple. There were two readings at each synagogue service: a reading from the Law

(*Torah*) and a reading from the Prophets (*Nebiim*), which was called the *haphtarah*, or "conclusion," because it was read at the end of the service. The Torah was read continuously, one book after another. The readings were divided into units so that the readings at each meeting would pick up where the reading at the last had ended.[1] From early on the readings from the Prophets that referred to the Diaspora and God's promises for the future were often selected. Thus readings started with the duty of every Jew to follow the Law. It was through obedience to the Law that individuals grew in their identity as Jews. The readings from the Prophets helped Jews understand their captivity and provided a vision for their restoration in the future.

By the time of Jesus, the institution of the synagogue had been brought back to Palestine by returning Judeans and was a regular part of Jewish religious practice. Synagogue services multiplied such that in many places there were daily services with specified prayers and blessings to go with the lessons for each service. Even with the development of the lectionaries, however, synagogue practice was far from uniform. Local custom dictated, among other things, the schedule of services and weekly prayers as well as many, if not most, of the specific scripture passages to be read. Nevertheless, the general rule for reading the scrolls of scripture seems to have been largely universal. The Torah was read continuously from beginning to end with its sections carefully divided so that in almost all the synagogues it took one full year to read the whole Pentateuch. The *haphtarah* was read selectively, to correspond with various seasons or holy days such as Rosh Hashanah or Pentecost.

First-century Jews living in Palestine, then, had three foci of worship. The Temple was at the symbolic center. Temple worship was an intricate series of festivals and holy days marked out by the lunar calendar and observed with various sacrifices. Jews regularly faced toward the Temple whenever they prayed.

Second, Jews shared table fellowship, primarily rooted in the ancient custom of the Sabbath supper, which originated at home where Jewish religion had always been grounded.[2] By the first century, however, table fellowship among Jews had expanded beyond the boundaries of the household to include various purposive associations such as burial societies. These meals, characterized by the ritual blessing of bread and wine at the beginning and end of the meal, are usually designated as *Chaburoth*.[3]

Finally, the synagogue, with its regular and systematic round of reading, instruction, and prayer formed the third focus, and it was here as well as in the home that Jewish identity was formed by the repetition of God's history with the chosen people and God's promises to them.

Reading Scripture in the First Three Hundred Years

The earliest confessors of Jesus were Jews who understood themselves as Jews who knew that Jesus was Messiah, that he was risen from the dead and would return soon to establish God's Reign on earth as it was established in Heaven. They frequented the Temple, ate ritual meals together (at which they believed Jesus was somehow present), and attended synagogue.

In 70 C.E. the Temple was destroyed. As the crisis of Gentile inclusion in what had begun as a Jewish sect precipitated the emergence of "Christianity" from Judaism, both Jews and "Christians" were without a central focus of worship. What was left for both Jews and Jewish Christians was the meal and the synagogue service. At first the "Christians" formed something like alternative synagogues: meetings in which scripture was read and interpreted (cf. James 2:2). The focus of Christian worship moved from the Sabbath to Sunday, the day of the resurrection; a service of the Word was joined to the evolving Christian table-ritual and the Sunday Eucharist appeared. In this two-part service the assembly would recite prayers, listen to readings, and hear a sermon. Then bread and wine would be offered with a blessing that recalled Jesus' life, death, resurrection, and promised return. This pattern was clearly established by about 150 C.E. as Justin Martyr attests:

> And on the day called Sunday, all who live in cities or the country gather together in one place and the memoirs of the apostles or the writings of the prophets are read as long as time permits; then, when the reader has ceased, the president verbally instructs and exhorts to the imitation of these good things. Then we all rise together and pray, and as we have said before, when our prayers are ended, bread and wine and water are brought,[4] and the president in like manner offers prayers and thanksgivings according to his ability and the people assent, saying Amen; and there is distribution to each and a participation of that over which thanks have been given, and to those who are absent a portion is sent by the deacons.[5]

5

The first three hundred years of the church's life was marked by highly eschatological expectations. The first believers expected Christ to return very quickly to execute justice and usher in a new world. As Jesus' return was delayed and as the church was increasingly persecuted, Christian eschatology subtly shifted focus to the immanence of arrest and execution, though the hope for the Parousia remained. Thus until Constantine legitimized Christianity in the fourth century, Christians understood themselves as living in a seam in history. This world was about to pass away and the next world established. Christians saw history as transient; they were fixed on the near future. They "connected" to the story of Jesus because they, like him, faced arrest, humiliation, torture, and death. As we will see, this changed after Christianity began to emerge as the official religion of the Roman Empire.

Our historical evidence for reading practices in worship during this early period is scanty. It seems that Christians met during the week for reading and prayer apart from the Eucharist. Though we know that they read from the Old Testament and from Christian books and letters, many of which would eventually become part of the New Testament canon, we do not know exactly how these were read. Many scholars assume that since there are numerous commentaries on whole books of the Bible by early patristic writers, one can assume that these books were read publicly from beginning to end: *lectio continua*.[6] We can reasonably assume that there was a great deal of variety, both in what was read and how the readings were structured, depending on local custom. For example, in some places, the martyrdom accounts of regional saints were sometimes included in the Eucharistic readings.[7] G. G. Willis, for example, has proposed that it was local Bishops who decided what was to be read and when.[8] This sort of local determination would suggest a kind of continuity with first-century synagogue practice.

For their first three centuries, Christians celebrated Easter as the center of their identity and Sunday as the "weekly Easter," for it was the death and resurrection of Jesus above all else that was the founding event of the church. Thus it was that Christians began their Easter and Sunday observances on the preceding Saturday evening just as Jews celebrated Sabbath beginning at sundown on Friday. Probably the first readings that were specified for a particular time and that received nearly unanimous use throughout the second- and third-century church were the Old Testament readings for the Easter Vigil, the nightlong service that the baptized Christians held while they waited for the appearance of the newly baptized in their midst just before sunrise. These readings selectively spanned the whole history of God's people from creation, the fall, and all the other critical events of Old Testament history, including those prophecies that the church held were predictions of the incarnation of Jesus Christ. It goes without saying that a Gospel account of the resurrection would have been the principal reading at the Easter sunrise Eucharist, the culmination of the Vigil.

Excursus: The Daily Offices and the Lectionary

For years "liturgical" churches in the West read only two lessons each Sunday and these were arranged on a one-year cycle. Churches in the Reformed and free traditions, on the other hand, read Sunday scripture either topically or *lectio continua* in sustained series in order to expound the fuller meanings of the text. The reasons this disparity in approach to Sunday readings continued until the late twentieth century are complicated but have to do in part with the way scripture was used in daily forms of prayer apart from the Eucharist. To understand the rationale of the RCL and its relation to the Reformation traditions, it is useful to look at the history of the Daily "Office."

Early Christians inherited from Judaism the customs of praying at certain hours during the day and marking days of the week with fasts. For example, whereas Jews fasted on Mondays and Thursdays, Christians chose Wednesdays and Fridays (*Didache* 8:1). Daily prayers marked times of the day with petitions and set selections from the psalms. Evidence for the first three centuries is scarce, but it is probable that these "hours" were prayed individually or in families in some times and places and as a worshiping community in others. Hippolytus correlates the hours of prayer with the stages in Christ's passion and also gives evidence that there was communal "instruction in the word of God" (*Apostolic Tradition* 35-36). After the Peace of Constantine, as churches and cathedrals proliferated, "cathedral offices" marking the hours of the day, particularly morning, noon, and evening, developed as popular liturgies. Though in some places, such as Egypt, scripture was read in these services, they were based primarily on selected psalms, scriptural canticles, and hymns rather than extended reading. However, cathedrals did celebrate "vigils" on Saturday evenings and before major feasts such as Easter. These services often occupied much of the night and emphasized scripture readings that were germane to the feast.

7

At the same time, the monastic movement enjoyed an unprecedented upsurge in popularity. The monastic offices marking the hours of the day emphasized the psalms, though in many places, particularly Egypt, the monastic practice was to follow scripture readings with periods of silence and meditation. In these practices one can see different purposes. The cathedral office was intended for popular, communal participation in liturgical observances, whether these were the marking and sanctifying of mundane time or the reliving of some foundational Christian event. The monastic service had as its goal the formation of the individual soul in increasing perfection. This meant that the monastic, meditative use of scripture was different from the public, liturgical iterations, which were intended for the formation of communal memory and celebration, based in the ancient Christian conviction that "where two or three are gathered," Christ will be present (Matt 18:20).

In the fifth and sixth centuries more abundant evidence appears for readings, lectionaries, and even homilies in the offices and vigils of various cathedrals and in monastic hours. As Western medieval laypeople lost the ability to understand Latin, the proclamation of scripture in church became problematical for them. This was especially so since the Western church eventually adapted the Roman Sunday lectionary, which meant reading only two lessons. The Roman use was ordinarily a selection from the Epistles and a Gospel reading, using the same pericopes without variation every year. Although this system made it possible for nonliterate people to learn to associate certain Sundays with certain biblical texts, it radically reduced the amount of scripture exposed to people who attended only Mass.[9]

Nevertheless, the idea that the offices should be public liturgies in church continued through most of the medieval period. Multiple daily liturgies that included psalms, canticles, readings, and prayers arranged in a complicated fashion evolved. Often a consortium of churches would decide on sharing the round of services so that morning prayer would be done in one place, evening prayer in another, and so forth. In many places, particularly Spain, these services followed local custom and remained well attended. In the meantime, the Benedictine arrangement of the offices, with its systematic singing through of the psalter, gained monastic popularity.

Beginning in the eighth century the movement to make the Roman use universal throughout the Carolingian Empire meant that every church was supposed to celebrate all the offices. By the eleventh century this reform meant that it was the obligation of all clergy to recite communally all the offices daily. This proved impractical for pastoral and logistical reasons. Therefore, clergy were often dispensed and allowed to say the offices by themselves. To facilitate this, the numerous books used for monastic services, such as the psalter, the lectionary, and the collectionary, had to be distilled into one book, which clergy could carry with them and from which all the offices could be read. These books were called "breviaries," and all clergy were expected to have and use them.

Throughout the medieval period the need to simplify the complicated Roman offices was in tension with the pressure to introduce more saints' days and more hagiographical readings into the offices at the expense of systematic exposure to the psalms and scripture. By the thirteenth century, European laypeople had lost almost all touch with the Daily Offices and turned instead to rich extra-liturgical devotional books, which by the fifteenth century were printed in the vernacular.

The Reform movements and the rise of humanism in the Late Middle Ages brought with them increased pressure to simplify the offices and make them vehicles of systematic exposure to Holy Writ. In 1535, acting with papal authorization, Cardinal Quinones of Spain introduced a radically reformed breviary. It eliminated all pretext of being a communal and choral book, which meant that the offices were presumed to be for the edification and formation of individual clergy. It was, in a sense, a triumph of the "monastic" model.

Quinones' breviary provided for the reading of all 150 psalms every week, and biblical reading was planned so that the whole New Testament would be read each year. In order to accomplish this, it eliminated most of the saint's days. The experiment proved unpopular because it divorced daily prayer from the church year. Nevertheless, it brought into sharp focus the difficulty of reconciling broad exposure to scripture with a one-year Eucharistic lectionary cycle that included only two readings.

Luther wanted to purge the liturgy of anything that suggested "works" and was intent on ensuring that the people would hear the gospel of salvation by grace through faith at the center of all services. He retained the breviary offices of matins, vespers, and compline, simplified them, and sought to restore them as the main public services on weekdays. In this way he seems to have meant to return to the cathedral offices. However, he changed the nature of these liturgies by providing that scripture was read and preached. He thus replaced the ancient notion of daily prayer and praise offered to God with a proclamation of God's mercy toward humankind. In this he was theologically consistent in his insistence that we have nothing to offer to God and that liturgy is directed primarily at the congregation.

Variations of Luther's plan were installed in a number of churches and schools, but except for a few metropolitan centers these offices gradually fell into disuse, falling victim to the Protestant sense that the home was the spiritual center of Christian prayer.

The Reformed tradition also retained morning and evening prayer, and these were widely observed in Switzerland and other Reformed areas. Like Luther's liturgies, these were services of the word. In Strasbourg and elsewhere, the service consisted mainly of psalms said or sung metrically and long sections of scripture *lectio continua*. The conviction that the plain, systematic exposition of Holy Writ was the center of Christian worship meant the demise of the church year and a corresponding lectionary.

In England, Cranmer's *Book of Common Prayer* continued the Roman use of a one-year set cycle of Epistles and Gospels for the Eucharist. This meant that the Daily Office would bear the responsibility of the systematic exposition of Scripture. Cranmer conflated the medieval offices into matins and Evensong. Though he simplified the structure, he retained many of the ancient elements of praise and supplication in a way that encouraged the development of a unique choral tradition. On the reform side, he provided that the psalms and the Bible be read *lectio continua*. Thus, unlike the Reformed tradition, Cranmer was able to retain the church year and also provide for systematic public Bible reading. It was directed that these offices be said or sung in every church in England, and it is a tribute to the quality of Cranmer's solution that this practice was widely followed for hundreds of years.

The Council of Trent sought to reform the office to make it easier to read while maintaining the basic medieval structure. Thus the offices were to remain primarily a private, clerical obligation until the reforms of Vatican II.

The twentieth century seems to have witnessed two decisions on the part of "liturgical" churches. The first was that the normative Sunday service should be the ancient pattern of a service of the word followed by a service of the table and that this assembly should be the primary locus of the exposition of God's Word. Further, it was assumed that this Sunday assembly should be in the rich setting of the church year. To this end there has been consensus that the old Roman two-lesson, one-year cycle should be replaced with a lectionary system that uses three readings and a psalm portion arranged in a multiyear schedule in order to insure reading most of the Bible. The *Revised Common Lectionary* is an ecumenical response to these decisions.[10]

Constantine and the Christian Identity Crisis

A Sunday visitor who went to church in Rome in the year 450 (just a little over a hundred years after Constantine made Christianity a legal religion) would have been part of an impressive service. Hundreds of people would be packed into a very large, high, and long "basilica." The altar at the east end would have been high on a platform, and a long, elevated runway-aisle with low walls running the length of the building would lead up to it. People would be singing hymns, psalms, and prayer litanies as they gathered for the service. Then, at the appointed time, the choir would leave the altar area and join other ministers at the back of the church for the procession. The procession would enter with everyone singing, "I will go to the altar of God, even the God of my joy and gladness." The procession would be led by a swinging, billowing censer, followed by multiple torches, acolytes, choir, subdeacons, deacons, and priests all clothed in vestments distinctive to their order. The deacon would enter, carrying on a white cloth the richly bound, ornate, jewel-encrusted book of the Gospels. He would be followed by the archdeacon and finally the bishop, who would come slowly, reaching out and blessing people as he made his way to the altar.

The long service that would follow would include the same elements that Justin Martyr described three hundred years before, but now almost everything would be sung, and there would be numerous processions for everything from prayers, to readings, to bringing up the offerings of bread and wine and for Communion. The readings themselves were now determined in advance for every Sunday. They were sung, and the Gospel was accorded special reverence, both as text and in the presentation of the book itself:

> After the deacon returns from singing the Gospel, the subdeacon, who held the book during the reading of the gospel, receives the "evangeliary" and holding it up, follows the other subdeacon in procession. Then, holding the book near his heart on the outside of his vestment, he opens it so that it may be kissed by all the various grades of clergy who are standing in the sanctuary according to the order of their rank.[11]

The sermon that followed the reading of the Gospel would be given by the bishop from his raised *cathedra*, or throne-like chair behind the altar. Typically, it would address the Gospel and other lessons of the day, the time of the church year, and often some important point of doctrine.[12]

How did such a great ceremonial elaboration of the liturgy happen in such a relatively short time? Within 150 years the church had designated lessons for every Sunday between what would come to be called Advent and Pentecost as well as for every feast day.[13] Moreover, the various readings were now found in separate books. The book containing the Gospels, sometimes in full with the pericopes for each Sunday marked and sometimes containing only the designated readings, was itself accorded the kind of reverence given to sacred relics and the Eucharist. The change in ethos of the liturgy, including the liturgy of the word, signaled a subtle but deep shift in the way people understood what it meant to be a Christian.

In the 250 years preceding Constantine, Christians understood themselves to be misunderstood and persecuted in a world that was temporarily dominated by the power of evil. The cosmic powers that had crucified Jesus continued to rage against his people so that although Christians lived "in the world" yet they were not "of the world." By the early fourth century, becoming a Christian meant undergoing a long process, which involved, among other things, forsaking any profession that was involved with Roman civil government or religion. Aspirants were observed and catechized for three years before finally, after much fasting and praying, they were initiated on Easter Eve in an all-night service that included exorcisms, renunciation of the powers of this world, nude baptismal immersion, vesting in a clean white garment, chrismation, reception by the bishop, and first Communion.[14]

By participating in this enormous preparation and liturgy, a Christian renounced his or her citizenship in the Roman world and became a citizen of the kingdom of God. It was, in the profoundest sense, a change in identity. From the time of initiation on, the Christian communed with other Christians in this world and eventually in heaven: to be a Christian was to know oneself as already a citizen of the next world and a stranger in this one. The political power and imperial pomp that was the glory of this world was shame to the Christian. And, likewise, what was considered shameful in this world, weakness and subjection, was glory to the siblings of the Crucified One. Christians needed only to remain faithful in the communion of the church to be certain of salvation at death.

12

When Constantine became emperor, however, the image of Christians as persecuted outsiders changed dramatically. Christians were soon invited into the halls of power as their faith was tolerated and indeed promoted throughout the empire. Old bishops, who bore the crippling scars of Roman torture, found themselves convened by the emperor to make official theological decisions about the nature of Christ at the Council of Nicaea in 325. Some of them could so scarcely believe their newfound status that they wondered if God's kingdom had already come! At the inspiration of St. Helena, the emperor's mother, the Holy Land was soon dotted with new churches and shrines commemorating various events in the life of Christ. The supposed "true cross" on which the Lord had died was unearthed and enshrined at the new Church of the Holy Sepulcher in Jerusalem, built at the site of Jesus' interment. All over the empire large new churches were being built, and the Eucharist was celebrated with increased uniformity and ceremony. The relics of martyrs, which had always been revered by Christians, were now in great demand and were being "translated" from their original burial sites to places beneath the altars of churches. Those who could afford it began making pilgrimages to the Holy Land to be a part of groups that, led by clergy, went from site to site "reliving" the events of Jesus' life. At each "station" there seems to have taken place a kind of service in which, among other things, portions of Prophets and the Gospels appropriate to that site were read. A new way was being made for Christians to participate in the events on which their faith was founded.

One of Constantine's motives for elevating the status of Christianity and commissioning new religious shrines within the empire was unifying the realm and legitimizing his reign. The church was to become an imperial institution. This implied a triumphalist theology in which the aims of the emperor and of God were seen to be the same; the coming of the Christian empire was part of God's plan of salvation. As such both the theology and the liturgy had to be uniform so as to mediate the unity of the empire. Ecumenical councils convened during this time were concerned with unifying the church's doctrine and the liturgy. As a result lessons for many major feasts were standardized.[15]

Some changes were pragmatic. Now that being a Christian was not only tolerated throughout the empire but had social and political advantages, large numbers of people sought baptism. The church had difficulty deciding on how to handle the rush of aspirants, both because of logistics and because it feared diluting a believer's fervency. Its first solution was to insist on continuing a long period of catechesis and testing before initiation. During this time the catechumens received lengthy instruction in the Christian life based on the liturgy and scripture. Some of the earliest commentaries on the Bible were written for these catechumens waiting to be baptized.

Even though in the fourth and fifth centuries many parents, such as those of St. Augustine, elected to delay baptism till the intemperance of youth had ebbed, the increasing numbers of those already baptized, together with those who attended church without baptism, necessitated large churches and a liturgy suited to those grand spaces.

But pragmatism and the imperial desire for uniformity are not sufficient to explain the liturgical evolution that was underway. Another, more important reason, internal to the Christian faith itself, was in operation. It involved a new notion of what it meant to *be* a Christian and what Christians meant by salvation.

Before Constantine, Christians understood themselves to be a pure and holy people who belonged to the world to come. Salvation was a matter of remaining a faithful member of the church until death or until Jesus returned for the final judgment. Minor sins were matters for reconciliation within the church. Major sins, such as murder, which would bring shame and condemnation on the church, however, resulted in excommunication, and this meant spiritual death.[16] Simply put, the church was a visible community without serious sin, a pure and holy people, and outside the church there was no salvation.

After Constantine, something basic changed. Although the church struggled to preserve the rigorous process of selection and formation for initiation that would guarantee its continued purity, this proved impossible. First, Constantine's extension of tolerance throughout the empire meant an end to the social pressure of public contempt and persecution that enabled Christians to think of themselves as victims whose destiny was victory. Instead, Christians were set up as the models of public virtue and given power and prestige. Second, the sheer number and diversity of the baptized as well as the *illuminandi*—those prepared for baptism but "holding off" till they matured—made the old strict discipline impossible. Finally, as infant baptism became the norm, raising a large number of children to conform to the standards of a "pure" community became untenable.

Thus, after the middle of the fourth century, baptism no longer signaled as dramatic a change in identity for most people as it formerly had.

Clearly, in the case of infants it was not experienced as abruptly transformative. Instead of a community of the pure and holy, the church was now a mixture of individuals: some exceedingly pure, not a few scoundrels, and the vast majority ordinary people. No longer anxious about persecution and martyrdom, most churchgoers worried about things like child discipline, business decisions, erotic temptation, and the like. In other words, Christian life was very much like pagan life, and for the first time questions like "What difference does baptism make, anyway?" became central. The theology that evolved in these circumstances no longer saw salvation as a disjunctive moment in which one changed "citizenship" from this world to the next. Rather, the next world was a destination, and baptism was the beginning of the pilgrimage.

Baptism was still of fundamental importance for Christians: it remained the sacramental mystery in which one died and rose with Christ and was reborn. But this rebirth had a different nuance. At least in the West, the doctrine of original sin as developed by St. Augustine came to form the basis for the early medieval understanding of baptism. According to this account, we are all born of Adam's stock and are therefore inheritors of his guilt. Consequently, we justly inherit death. Christ came, however, to give us life and save us from Adam's fate. He did this by becoming one with Adam's stock and suffering Adam's due death without having sinned himself. Thus when he rose victorious over death, he opened the way of eternal life to humankind. In baptism we are joined with him in that new life.

The existential fact remained, however, that Christians continued to sin after baptism; some to greater or lesser degree, but all continued in sin. Baptism removed the inherited guilt, the *poena*, or penalty due from Adam's offspring, but it did not eliminate the inherent tendency to sin. Life after baptism was, therefore, a time of opportunity to grow in love, through the grace of God, until one was able to stand in the full presence of God. It was assumed that unless one was in fact free from sin, one would be unable to accept and enter into the fullness of the divine, unguarded, self-giving love of God. The Western church called this final, perfect relationship with God the "beatific vision" whereas the East boldly called it "divinization" (*theosis*). Later theologians would try to address these issues of the baptismal remission of original sin and progress in love by distinguishing between "justification" and "sanctification."

These sea changes in the way the church, baptism, and salvation were understood led to the development of the church year as a means by which Christians could grow in grace. The church year became the means by which an ordinary Christian participated over and over again in the events of his or her salvation. In the context of the year, the liturgy became both formation in Christ and access to the mysteries of salvation. It is to the formation and shape of that calendar that we now turn.

CHAPTER TWO

THE CHURCH YEAR: THE CHRISTIAN'S HISTORY

A s we have noted, the early church celebrated Sunday, Easter, and Pentecost. Easter and Pentecost supplanted the Jewish feasts of Passover and Pentecost and were now filled with the new Christian significance of Christ's resurrection and the gift of the Holy Spirit. As with their Jewish antecedents, the timing of these feasts changed from year to year calculated by the lunar calendar. Sunday, the "first day of the week" was celebrated weekly as a "little Easter," since it was the day of Christ's resurrection.

Beyond observing the anniversaries of the "birthdays into eternity" of martyrs, Christian gatherings did not seem to mark any historical occasions except the resurrection and the advent of the Spirit. This is because, as we have suggested, for the first three hundred years of its life the church lived as an eschatological community. The expectation of Jesus' imminent return and then the realities of persecution combined to focus Christian attention on the "now." One lived as a Spirit-possessed sibling of the risen Christ and anticipated only the immediate future in which the final trial and end would come. After Constantine, the eschatological tension abated and Christians, especially the newly converted, whose quotidian lives often continued without much change, began to ask, "What difference does Christianity make?" We have seen how the post-Constantinian theology of salvation changed from a disjunctive break with "this world" to a notion of spiritual pilgrimage toward a full and perfect vision of God. Now, part of this spiritual journey had to be made in this world, in ordinary day-to-day life. The process of sanctification to eternity had to take place in Ordinary Time. The question was how to make this everyday human existence a vehicle for sanctification, that is, how to make Ordinary Time sacred.

In the late fourth century, a Spanish nun named Egeria took a three-year pilgrimage from Egypt to the Holy Land during which she wrote a detailed diary for the edification of her sisters back home. Her aim was to visit holy sites that had figured in the history of the salvation of Israel and Christians. She gave a particularly vivid account of what she and other pilgrims experienced in Jerusalem from the Sunday before Easter to sunrise on Easter day. On what would eventually be called "Palm Sunday" the pilgrims, together with clergy, entered the city singing in procession, carrying branches. As they went, the people of the city greeted them and sang with them. The week was spent visiting and holding services at the various places where Scripture and tradition said that Jesus had been on that particular day and at that particular time. Thus, Thursday night was spent at the traditional site of the inn where Jesus had the "Last Supper" and in the garden of Gethsemane.

After this all-night vigil the pilgrims went in procession to the sites of Jesus' humiliation and sentencing. Then they walked the route to Golgotha, pausing on the way for readings and prayers at the various places where Scripture and tradition suggested that Jesus paused on that sad way. Finally, they spent three hours at Golgotha, after which they all returned to their lodgings and kept silence until the Saturday evening vigil at the Church of the Holy Sepulcher. There, following an all-night service of readings and prayer, when the morning star was sighted, the Eucharist began and proceeded as the sun rose. Egeria comments in a number of places on the appropriateness of the scripture readings for each time and commemorated event.

In retrospect, what was taking place is very clear. Egeria and pilgrims like her were finding a way to connect to their collective past by a kind of mimetic "reliving" of the foundational events of their faith. Like Judaism, Christianity is a faith grounded in history; events that really happened to real people in particular times and places. Although the Son of God, Jesus, was a Jew who was born of a certain mother, and who lived, died, and rose again in a certain area at a certain time, his history is the "family history" of every Christian. Just as being in the presence of the relic of one of the saints was to be in touch with a tangible bit of the life of an actual person who suffered martyrdom, so visiting the garden where Jesus waited for his arrest was to participate in that event and claim it as part of one's own history and identity.

Obviously, not even a monastic could spend a whole life visiting and revisiting the places of a Christian's foundational history. Even more important, the vast majority of Christians could not go the Holy Land to visit the sites of Jesus' life or to "revisit" the historical events that occurred there.[1] The challenge, then, was how to bring those events and those scenes to those believers who could not visit those locations in person. The elaboration of the church year was the result of this urge to participate in the founding events of Christianity and, in particular, the events of Christ's life, death, and resurrection.

The Paschal Cycle

The first part of the church year to develop took shape around what had always been the center of Christian celebration: the resurrection. Since by the third century there already was a long period of preparation for baptism culminating in an all-night vigil and the Easter Eucharist, it was not difficult to adapt the week before Easter into a mimetic observance of the events leading up to Jesus' resurrection. The Sunday preceding Easter was marked by reenacting Jesus' entry into Jerusalem, and the following week was filled with liturgical observances. The culmination of the week, the events from the "Last Supper" on Thursday to the resurrection on Sunday, comprised a single piece of salvation history that came to be known as the *triduum* ("three days").[2] It is precisely these events that Egeria detailed in the fourth century. The *triduum* became the core of the Lenten season and the "Great Fifty Days" of Easter.

The first "season" to be established was the time between Easter and Pentecost, which corresponded to the Jewish "holy feast of seven weeks" between Passover and the "feast of the first fruits" (see Tobit 2:1). It was seen as a time in which Jesus was present on earth, so a fifty-day long Easter in which no fasting or kneeling was permitted.[3]

By the end of the fourth century, Ascension Day was established on the fortieth day after Easter. This overcame some disagreement about its historical location since Luke (24:50) implies that Christ ascended on

Easter. It also characterized it as a discrete event that could be, like Easter and Pentecost, "relived" liturgically. Furthermore, it helped distinguish Pentecost as the Feast of the Holy Spirit, which was now provided with its own vigil. As such, Pentecost became the culmination of the salvation history narrative of the church year.

The time before Easter had always been a time of increased prayer both by candidates for initiation and the church members who prayed for them. Pre-Easter fasting, however, only lasted a few days. By the early fourth century a period of forty days became customary.[4] The number forty was most likely based on Israel's forty years in the wilderness and Jesus' forty-day fast in the wilderness. It also provided a nice symmetry with the forty days between Easter and Ascension. These forty days of fasting were counted differently depending on whether one fasted on Saturday or included Sunday, a day on which no one fasted, within the period. It was not until the seventh century that the present Western practice of starting Lent on a Wednesday to make up for the non-fasting Sundays was adapted.

From the early fifth century, Lent became the time in which those who were going to undertake a period of penance as part of the developing system of canonical penance made their ritual confession and put on the clothing of a penitent. This donning of sackcloth, which they would typically wear until Holy Week the following year, was accompanied by smearing their foreheads with ashes. It soon became customary for the clergy to take ashes along with the penitents as an act of solidarity. By the ninth century when canonical penance was largely replaced by repeatable, private confession, Lent had become a time for yearly, personal penance by all Christians, and everyone received ashes. Thus the beginning of Lent came to be "Ash Wednesday."

Lent also became a yearly period for intensification of those things that might move a Christian on toward perfection: fasting, confession, prayer, almsgiving, and reparation towards one's neighbors. Thus the "paschal cycle," the time beginning with Ash Wednesday and culminating with Pentecost, developed as a way of "reliving" the foundational events of Christian identity: Jesus' passion, death, and resurrection, followed by the gift of the Holy Spirit. These, of course, were not the only foundational events of the Christian narrative. Completing the year required another "cycle."

The Incarnational Cycle

The evolution of the church season that begins with Advent and ends with the presentation of Christ in the Temple on February 2 was complex. Advent itself was the last church season to develop. The fourth and fifth centuries witnessed an intensified interest in the birth of Christ. This was partly because this era was occupied with the orthodox struggle with Arianism. The need to defend the divinity of Jesus led the church to emphasize the Incarnation of the Son of God both as a doctrine and an object of devotion. Even more important, however, was the soteriology of the period, which emphasized that by becoming incarnate in Jesus Christ, God had redeemed sinful human nature and made it possible for humanity to achieve the beatific vision. Indeed, it was this notion of salvation that required the defeat of Arianism. So Christmas was understood not only as the birth of Jesus; it was the Feast of the Incarnation, and reliving it liturgically became a way of entering into a central mystery of Christian salvation.

The situation of Christmas in the calendar is another matter. It is likely that the Feast of the Epiphany on January 6 was actually celebrated before Christmas per se and that it included not only the visit of the magi but the birth itself. Furthermore, there is also evidence that something like an Epiphany season existed in the East by the end of the third century, though not in the West until the early fifth. During this season texts that manifested Jesus' identity as the Christ, such as the accounts of Jesus' baptism and the wedding miracle at Cana, were read. What began as a time that simultaneously celebrated both Jesus' birth and manifestation as Christ became divided into two separate seasons, each commemorating different aspects of Christian salvation history.

The division of Epiphany into two seasons is an example of the same phenomenon witnessed in the placing of Ascension forty days after Easter; Christians were now able to relive them as distinct liturgical events. As Christian initiation began to be celebrated at times other than at the Vigil of Easter, Epiphany became a preferred time for baptisms, perhaps because of the old custom of reading the account of Jesus' baptism in that season.

The celebration of Christmas on December 25 is first documented in Rome in 336 and in the East at the beginning of the fifth century. Conventional liturgical wisdom maintained for years that December 25 was fixed as the date for Christmas in order to "Christianize" the pagan

21

winter solstice feast of *Sol Invictus*. Recent scholarship has suggested otherwise, however. Many rabbis argued that prophets died on the same date they were conceived. Through a linking of the date of Passover with the solar Julian calendar of the empire, some Christians in Asia Minor concluded that Jesus had been crucified on March 25, meaning that was also the date of his conception. Hence, December 25 was reckoned as his birth date.[5]

Through the fourth and fifth centuries other events associated with Jesus' birth gained places in the liturgical calendar. Beginning in the fifth century, December 28 was commemorated as the flight of the Holy Family into Egypt and the slaughtering of the "Holy Innocents" by Herod. Though the Feast of the Holy Name (Jesus' *bris*) on January 1 or 2 was of early medieval origin, the Feast of the Presentation of Christ in the Temple in February, forty days after Christmas, dates at least from the fourth century. Our old friend Egeria compares its celebration in Jerusalem to that of Easter! By the early seventh century the feast was being called "Candlemas" and was marked by blessing, lighting, and processing with the candles, which would then be used in church and in homes for the duration of the year. Thus in the medieval calendar it came to be a "Festival of Light" in the dark European February, emphasizing the theme of Christ as the Light born into a dark world.

The first part of the incarnational cycle moved from Jesus' birth through his flight from Herod and his circumcision. Then it moved back to Bethlehem and the newborn Child to include Matthew's account of the Epiphany. For the next several Sundays various stories manifesting Jesus' identity were read. Since the middle of the twentieth century, the story of the Transfiguration, read on the last Sunday before Lent, culminated this cycle.[6] The reading of stories, some of the adult Jesus, is punctuated by the February 2 observance of the presentation of the infant Jesus in the Temple. Obviously, the chronology of this cycle looks confused. What appears to be a narrative of Jesus' early life from birth to the Transfiguration, the event after which Jesus sets his face toward Jerusalem and moves inexorably toward his passion, is interrupted by two feasts that return us to the infancy: Epiphany and the presentation. The church year was not planned by a committee of theologians, it grew as the expression of millions of Christians who wanted a way to connect to Christ, a way to have those historical events by which they were saved be present in their everyday lives. The Incarnation suggested two narrative themes: one the odyssey of Jesus' birth and childhood, the other the proclamation of his power and authority as the Christ. The two are related and overlap, but are not identical. In a sense, these two aspects of the church year suggest a tension inherent in the Incarnation itself. On one hand, Christ is fully human and on the other, fully divine. Expressing these mysteries simultaneously necessarily involves moving back and forth between the poles of human vulnerability and divine power. So in the midst of the Epiphany narration of Jesus' authority, Candlemas shows him appearing at the Temple in his mother's arms.

Liturgy is innately conservative. Feasts that have been celebrated on a certain date for centuries are not readily moved. So it is with the chronology of the Incarnation. The themes of Incarnation and Epiphany are intercalated, but the overarching trajectory of the calendar from Christmas to Lent is clear. Jesus, the divine Child, is born and as a human undergoes those rites of passage that any child of his culture would. As he lives and grows, his divine identity is manifest in what happens to him, because of him (the flight into Egypt, the slaying of the Innocents, the prophecy of Simeon, the voice at his baptism), and in his actions (changing water into wine, calling the disciples, teaching with authority). By living out liturgically the incarnational cycle and then the paschal cycle each year, the Christian could, and can today, encounter and live into the whole story of her or his salvation, week by week, in his or her parish church.

Ordinary Time

But the church year does not end there. Following the Feast of Pentecost, there are roughly six months of what we currently call "Ordinary Time."[7] The liturgical color associated with this period is neither solemn nor celebrative; it is green, the color of ongoing vegetative life. During Ordinary Time we read those parts of the Bible that instruct Christians on how to live out their baptisms.

In Ordinary Time we move from a recounting of the events of salvation to a rather open-ended season devoted to instruction. But the gospel typically refers to the final act of salvation history as a future event. The earliest Christians, following their Jewish understanding, thought of themselves as living at the end-time, just before Jesus' return at which he would judge the living and the dead and bring about a cosmic change that would mean the reign of God's peace, love, and everlasting life (the

Parousia). This was "linear" history. God created the world once, and Jesus came into it, died and rose once, and will return just once. The end of the story was yet to happen and would happen only once. The Creed of Nicaea is very clear: "and he shall come again with glory to judge both the living and the dead."

But as we can readily see, the church year as we have described it begins with Christ's birth and seems to end with Pentecost. Moreover, it recycles again and again, year after year. The cyclical calendar reflects a change in the notion of salvation that occurred when the pre-Constantinian idea of disjunctive salvation evolved into the notion of salvation as pilgrimage toward perfection. Repeating the narrative of salvation history over and over gave Christians a chance every year to grow more loving through each season each year.

But how does one who lives the church year get to that future time of judgment and peace? If we look at the RCL, we see a contemporary version of the pattern of reading that developed in the sixth and seventh centuries. The months that follow Pentecost do not immediately take us to the Parousia. Indeed, Ordinary Time seems to change the focus from the narrative of salvation to an exploration of the Bible, wherein whole sections are read at length over a span of Sundays. The clear connections between the Gospel readings and the other lessons largely disappear. Whereas in the incarnational and paschal cycles Bible passages were selected to tell the "story" of Christ (*lectio selecta*), in Ordinary Time it is read in more or less continuous selections (*lectio continua*) in order to explore the riches of the books themselves. So the emphasis falls on unpacking the richness of, say, Ephesians, rather than reliving the story of Jesus. In chapter 7 we will explore Ordinary Time in its own right.

For now it must be noted that Ordinary Time does not point us toward the Parousia. From sometime in May or early June until December, we almost seem to lose sight of the end-time except as it may come up in the course of reading an Epistle here or a Gospel story there. Yet the eschatological expectation and hope remain key to the Christian story. How, then, does the church year move from this rich but slightly meandering trajectory of Ordinary Time to the future time of judgment and peace? How does the worshiping community direct itself back to the narrative of salvation history? It became the task of Advent to answer that question.

Advent: The End and the Beginning

Advent makes its first recorded appearances as a penitential period before Christmas in fifth-century Europe. By the sixth century it had clearly become a season of preparation, particularly in Gaul and Spain. But the character of this preparation was strangely mixed, depending on geography. There are records of fasting for forty days before Christmas, but there is also evidence that it was seen as a joyous season, particularly in Rome. In many places, until the High Middle Ages, white vestments were worn and festal hymns sung. Indeed, in some medieval rites, such as the *Sarum* at Salsbury Cathedral in England and the Dominican Rite of Paris, Advent was observed neither in somber purple nor penitential sackcloth, but in blue, the color of the sky and of the Blessed Virgin Mary. Around the seventh century, the Parousia became a theme. Indeed, the *Dies Irae* ("Day of Wrath") may have originally been written for Advent![8] In medieval Jerusalem and some places in Europe, black became the color used for Advent. While by the middle of the sixth century it was becoming customary to fix Advent as the period of the four Sundays before Christmas, areas such as Gaul continued to observe a longer period of preparation. Many of the prayers for weeks before Christmas have a penitential tone and seem to portend judgment.

These different practices suggest that there were countervailing forces at work in the development of the Advent season. First, Christians came to honor Christmas by a few days of preparatory fasting, just as they already honored Easter and Pentecost. Second, preparation for Christmas was characterized by joyful anticipation of the Lord's Incarnation. But to the early Christians it also carried the jubilant anticipation for the Parousia. These were people who were, for the most part, convinced of their eternal destiny with God and so could look eagerly for his Second Coming.

As the notion of Salvation changed over time, however, later Christians were less certain of the future. Salvation was now contingent on making spiritual progress, on becoming less sinful and more loving. In this view, judgment took place at the time of one's death and the "saved" were assigned to a place of waiting, of continued opportunity for improvement or of purgation. At the Parousia, then, the waiting soul would be reunited with the body for final, everlasting joy. Some souls were perfect enough at death that they were able to be in the full presence of God immediately. Unlike these saints, however, at death the vast majority of

Christians would either be damned or accepted and consigned to the appropriate state for continuing improvement.

This new understanding carried with it heightened anxiety about judgment and salvation. The earlier, more Jewish notions of Jesus' judgment at the Parousia were conflated with the idea of his judgment "at the hour of our death." This perspective meant that for each believer, the eschaton was always as close as one's own death. Particularly as medieval people struggled through the chaos of the dissolution of the Roman Empire and the arduousness that constituted European life till at least the year 1000, it seemed clear that sin and death were active, powerful forces against which the Christian had to constantly strive. Thus Advent became a preparation for judgment and as such sounded the sober chords of self-examination and penitence. Violet and black were not inappropriate colors from this point of view!

Advent was assigned a dual task. On one hand, an essentially linear, historical view of salvation had to be reconciled with the liturgical experience of reliving the events of salvation history over and over, year after year. On the other, the somber themes of sin and judgment had to be put together with the joyous themes of Christian assurance and the good news of the Incarnation. The solution was to begin Advent by emphasizing in prayer and reading, the themes of sin and judgment and then subtly turn toward joyful anticipation as Christmas approached, appearing to almost turn the Second Coming into a celebration of the First. We will look at how this task is accomplished in the current *Revised Common Lectionary* in chapter 5, though it is interesting to note at this point that in the readings that are designated for the Sundays at the end of Ordinary Time, the RCL begins to anticipate Advent several weeks before the season begins in a manner not unlike the early medieval Gallican practices.

Since we have here introduced the notions of judgment at death and an "intermediate state" for the souls of the faithful, it may be helpful to add a word about a fourth element of the church calendar: the sanctoral cycle.

The Sanctoral Cycle

As we have seen, early medieval Christians, who viewed salvation as what later theologians would call "sanctification," understood that probably most souls needed to spend further time after death being formed in the mind of Christ. This had seemed clear to many even before the fourth century. In the second century, Clement of Alexandria suggested that deathbed converts, who had no time to do penitential works in this life, would be purified by fire in the next.[9] This notion was combined with the very early Christian beliefs that the prayers of the living could influence the fate of the dead[10] and that martyrs who were received into heaven immediately remained in community with their brothers and sisters and continued to pray for them.

It was the custom of the early church to observe the anniversary of a martyr's "birthday into eternity" and to venerate his or her relics. The custom of celebrating Eucharist at the graves of martyrs is well attested in North Africa and Rome. After Constantine, when many relics were being translated and given new homes in churches for which they were "patrons," the regular observation of saints' days entered the church's calendar. These celebrations then combined with customary observances of significant people that were actually part of the narrative cycles of Incarnation and Pasch, such as the birth of John the Baptist, the death of the Evangelist Mark, and the dormition of the Blessed Virgin Mary. As it evolved, this sanctoral cycle called for a list of readings thought to be appropriate to the lives and deaths of particular saints. Unfortunately, it grew in such a way that by the High Middle Ages it tended to obscure the trajectories of some of the church year. Although since saints' days were "movable" feasts, they never replaced the major observations of the calendar.

Even though the sanctoral cycle was very important to the medieval church and continues to be important in the Roman Catholic and Anglican Communion's celebrations such as All Saints' Day and the Feast of St. Mary the Virgin, it has always been in some tension with the church year. This tension continues today in the *Revised Common Lectionary* and in the efforts of Anglicans, Lutherans, and United Methodists to produce ancillary liturgical calendars that would acknowledge the ongoing work of the Holy Spirit in Christian history. Even so, the RCL's existence stands as a reminder that the church includes all the saints of all times and cultures, past, present, and future, and that these, our brothers and sisters, continue in eternal communion with us.

THE LECTIONARY AS HERMENEUTIC

Hermeneutics has been a matter of much philosophical and theological attention for the past fifty years or so. Of course, hermeneutics has a much longer history than that. For centuries it had a fairly narrow and focused meaning: the principles by which the exegete interpreted Scripture. Thus, for instance, Alexandrian biblical interpreters, typified by Origen, looked for the "spiritual" meaning of scripture by the hermeneutic of allegory, whereas interpreters in Antioch tended to interpret biblical texts with more attention to historical events. Developed medieval hermeneutics taught that all scripture had four levels of meaning: the literal, the moral, the doctrinal, and the mystical or eschatological, which spoke of the final destiny of creation.

Since the nineteenth century, hermeneutics has been used in an expanded sense to refer to the process and presuppositions underlying the way each person "makes sense" out of the manifold aspects of his or her experience. The positivist assumption that one can simply know facts, whether about nature or history, has been confuted by the realization that every perception of an event is already an interpretation based on previous experience and presuppositions about the makeup of reality. Those presuppositions themselves are the result of the way in which an individual has "learned" to make sense out of reality and the assumptions of the various communities to which she or he belongs. For instance, a person who has grown up in a household that discounts what might be called the "supernatural," who has been trained in a rather positivist "scientific" approach to reality, and who belongs to a church community that tends to see Christianity primarily as a moral system and Jesus as a great teacher would tend to see the unexpected and medically inexplicable recovery of a dying spouse quite differently from a person whose family and religious community believed in the possibility of "supernatural intervention" in life and who understood Jesus as the divine God incarnate. Two quite different but yet "Christian hermeneutics" would produce quite different interpretations. Thus the same two people would probably interpret the biblical accounts of the resurrection quite differently.

This suggests that one of the ways to look at Christianity is as a "hermeneutic." The gospel helps Christians to "make sense" out of reality. At the same time, it also means that how this or that Christian in his or her community understands the gospel influences how that sense-making turns out. This is the reason that every good preacher knows intuitively that preaching has far more to do with expanding the horizons of hermeneutical presuppositions than it does with making rational arguments.

The Church Year and the Lectionary

This intuition was a driving force behind the formation of the Christian year. We saw in the preceding two chapters that the formation of the Christian year was in large part a response to the post-Constantinian shift in Christian identity. Multitudes of people were being baptized and found that their lives continued without much change. The liturgical year was a way that Christians, year by year, could relive the foundational events of the gospel while continuing in the necessary ordinariness of their work and family. In this process, in the validating matrix of the church in which other Christians were sharing the same story, the Christian's hermeneutic, his or her presuppositions about reality, expanded to include the reality of God's love and redemption. The implicit hermeneutical strategy of the liturgical year was the repetitive reliving of the foundational events of Christianity at the core of which were the life of Jesus Christ and the gift of the Holy Spirit at Pentecost. This liturgical reliving was meant to form a way of framing all the quotidian events of life such that God's grace and the claim of God's love could be known as the beginning and end of it all.

The first part of every Eucharist, Sunday by Sunday and season by season, was the liturgy of the word, in which lessons were read, portions of the psalter were sung, and a sermon was given. These readings gradually came to be closely coordinated with the season of the year, as were the words of the prayers, the hymns, the colors of the vestments used, and so on, so that the whole liturgy surrounded the worshiper with the sense of the events of that particular time in the sacred Christian cycle.

The reading customs of the first and second centuries admitted a good deal of variety among the locally chosen lessons, but always rested on the base of Hebrew Scripture, that is, the Old Testament. Eventually, as the New Testament canon was established, the readings for the two "cycles" became more stable, beginning with the very old set of lessons for Holy Week and the Easter Vigil.

Our *Revised Common Lectionary* continues to honor those very ancient selections such as John 13 for Maundy Thursday in every year, but seeks to establish an overall plan that reads the salient parts of the whole New Testament in a three-year cycle. This scheme finds its anchor in reading Matthew, Mark and, Luke in years A, B, and C respectively, while reading portions of John in each of the three years. This means that in any year the Synoptic "take" on the Gospel is always balanced with the Johannine one.

The arrangement of the readings is as follows:

1. Old Testament selection, occasionally a New Testament reading (that is, Acts in Easter)
2. A Psalm portion
3. A New Testament lesson other than a Gospel reading, most often an Epistle
4. A Gospel reading

The internal "logic" of this scheme during the first half of the year, that is, from Advent through Pentecost, is that the Old Testament reading and the psalm are chosen for their commensurability with the Gospel reading. This is based on the Christian hermeneutical principle, established by the time of Irenaeus, that the two Testaments constituted a unity. This unity had traditionally been understood to mean that everything in the Old Testament has a double meaning. On one hand, it refers in its own time to God's dealings with Israel. On the other hand, it refers either by typology or by outright prediction to Christ and the church as the New Israel. The disadvantage in this arrangement is that the Hebrew Bible has very little chance of being explored in its own right for its insights on God's dealing with us. It also lends itself to a "successionist" theology, which in our post-Holocaust era is really untenable for Christians. This is somewhat rectified in Ordinary Time, which we shall discuss below.

The third reading also usually relates to the Gospel, though sometimes this relationship is less obvious than others. For instance, the third readings in the Sundays of Easter are clearly related to Jesus' death, resurrection, and glorification, whereas in the Sundays after Epiphany the lessons from the Epistles seem to pick up their own themes. Thus it is clear that the idea is to lead the worshiper through the events of Christ's life, death, and resurrection based on the Gospel accounts with the rest of scripture playing a largely supporting role.

From Pentecost until the Sunday before Advent (often identified as Christ the King Sunday), the church year designates Ordinary Time. It is often put that the "Narrative Time" tells us of how God has dealt, is dealing, and will deal with us, while Ordinary Time tells us how we should respond. On the face of it, this bit of catechesis is a good starting place to explore the church year. For one thing, it includes two of the most important "uses" the church has always found for scripture: the retelling of the Christian story and the implications of that story for living a Christian life. It also helps explain why the lessons of Ordinary Time are arranged a bit differently from those of Narrative Time. From Advent to Pentecost, all readings, especially those of the Old Testament, work back from the Gospel. In Ordinary Time, the Old Testament lessons are far less likely to pair off in this way and rather long sections of those readings as well as Epistle and Gospel lessons are presented in sequence so that for several Sundays in a row the worshiper will follow two or three biblical books *lectio continua*.

This encourages a somewhat different hermeneutical approach in Ordinary Time. Here the preacher is presented with the opportunity, for instance, to explore Paul's great Epistle to the Romans for sixteen consecutive Sundays in the summer of Year A. It also provides for a few particularly provocative texts to appear twice, once in Narrative Time, where the typological agenda is clear and again in Ordinary Time, where the texts can be explored in their own right. Thus the story of Abraham's willingness to sacrifice his son Isaac (Gen 22:1-19) appears as part of the Easter Vigil, where it clearly must be seen in the paschal context of Christ's sacrifice and again as part of Proper 8, Year A. There its only other "connection" would seem to be with the theme of faith that appears in the Romans readings throughout this period in Year A, but actually does not appear explicitly in the Proper 8 Epistle (Rom 6:12-23). Thus Ordinary Time provides the chance to do the kind of expository preaching that characterized not only much early church catechesis but the great Reformed preaching traditions of the sixteenth century.

But the two-part church year is not really as simple as the preceding description suggests. Because the text that we are reading is the Bible, we encounter a hermeneutical complication involving the formation of the canon of scripture itself.

Reading from Different "Locations"

The Bible has a history, and some of that history is evident in the texts themselves. It is not only true that, for instance, 1 and 2 Timothy reflect a later, more institutionally developed moment in the history of the church than do Galatians or 1 Corinthians, but one can find internally intertwined threads of interpretation in single books. Look, for instance, at the parable of the good Samaritan (Luke 10:29-37). Luke sets the story in the context of a conversation with a "lawyer," which in turn is set in a section of the Gospel that has to do with how Christians are to comport themselves as this age nears its end. The lawyer asks what he must do to be saved, and Jesus gives him a perfectly good Judaic answer by quoting Torah (Deut 6:5, Lev 19:18b). When the lawyer asks who he must regard as neighbor, Luke has Jesus tell the parable. Luke's version ends with Jesus asking which of the three men in the story was a neighbor. When the lawyer identifies the Samaritan, Jesus says: "Go and do likewise."

For Luke, writing for a largely Gentile church that expected Jesus' Parousia, the parable of the good Samaritan is a teaching about how Christians should behave toward others. Of course, Luke did not make up the story. It undoubtedly came to him as part of the Christian tradition and had Palestinian origins. In that social setting the story would have been heard quite differently from the way Luke presents it. A first-century Palestinian Jew hearing the story would have noted first of all that being mugged on the road from Jerusalem down to Jericho was quite likely; it was a robber-infested area. Our Palestinian might also have appreciated the anti-clerical irony of the way in which the priest and the Levite ignored his plight. What would have been expected next was a Jewish "commoner," who might respond to the victim's plight, thus showing up

33

the clergy. But instead, a Samaritan, a person hated and despised by every Jew, a person who would have been expected to gloat over the poor Jew's plight, not only comes to his aid but extends his generosity beyond any reasonable expectation. The reaction of our hypothetical Jewish hearer might have been humiliation for the helpless victim, who was now sub-ject to the indignity of being at the mercy of a Samaritan, and anger that such an ingrained social stereotype was being challenged.

Now what we see is that Luke's parable of the good Samaritan includes at least two strands of interpretive "hearing," each dependent upon some-what different cultural and social-contextual settings. Luke's construal uses a traditional story that was probably familiar to Christians but that might have lost its "bite" in a Gentile community. Luke presents it to his Christian community as an exhortation to treat each other and their pagan neighbors with love and care, an especially difficult task in a world that was beginning to persecute Christians. The social contexts of the Palestinian Jew and the Gentile Christian are different, and so the same story becomes a quite different story when heard from each social "place."

When working with this lesson, the preacher has, in effect, at least two texts from which to choose. Neither can claim innate superiority over the other. Both are "in" Scripture. One enjoins love and care for others, a challenging characteristic of the Christian life, especially if one thinks of loving those who do not love back. The other, more elu-sive, might intimate that God's love is more radically inclusive than humans can imagine or that God's reign turns human social construc-tions upside down.

Since the good Samaritan appears in Ordinary Time (July 10-16, Year C), the preacher is under no special constraint either to relate this text to the other readings or to a particular liturgical time. But what if a text with a similar innate intertwining appears in one of the narrative cycles? Here the readings are probably all related to the Gospel and the Gospel in turn related to a particular "moment" in the church year. Such is the case with the parable of the prodigal son, which appears in Lent 4, Year C.

Here the parable is aligned with Joshua 5:9-12 in which the Lord tells Israel: "Today I have rolled away from you the disgrace of Egypt." The people celebrate Passover, the manna of the wilderness ceases, and they are established in a land of their own. The second reading, Psalm 32 begins, "Happy are those whose transgression is forgiven . . . to whom the LORD imputes no iniquity." This is followed by 2 Corinthians 5:16-21 in which we are told that if we are "in Christ, there is a new creation" and "All this is from God, who reconciled us to himself through Christ."

Clearly this Sunday, two weeks away from Palm Sunday, has reconciliation and forgiveness as its main themes. It is firmly anchored in the parable of the prodigal, which has traditionally been the great paradigm of reconciliation. It was, for instance, the favorite text of medieval preachers when they addressed the rite of reconciliation (confession).

In this liturgical context, it is important that the preacher remember that the trajectory of the Lenten season moves from fasting, self-denial, and the acknowledgment of sin to this promise of forgiveness in Lent 4 and then on to the promise of new life on the last Sunday in Lent (Lent 5). Lent becomes a season through which the traditional Christian pattern of salvation is lived: acknowledgment of sin (confession), reconciliation (forgiveness and restoration), and the promise of new, eternal life. All the readings of Lent 4 point to the prodigal as the paradigm of reconciliation. Thus it is virtually unavoidable that the Lent 4 preacher dedicate her or himself to the theme of reconciliation.

Yet the recognition of this theme creates, but does not limit, the theological and pastoral possibilities. For instance, it could be approached topically by pointing out, for instance, that the world needs reconciliation at every level from the alienated self to the nations and the environment and asking what needs to happen for this reconciliation to move forward. It could be approached dogmatically, outlining the steps of confession, promise of amendment, absolution, restitution if appropriate, and reconciliation. This could be framed psychologically, sacramentally, or even in terms of traditional ascetical theology. Or it could be approached by carefully exegeting one or more of the texts and making an exposition of, for instance, Paul's understanding of being "in Christ" or following the narrative of the prodigal's story of sin, separation, and restoration.

In any of these or other ways of coming to Lent 4, the preacher is attentive to the background of the season of Lent and its trajectory, which itself is only the first part of the paschal cycle. This means always standing in the storyline that leads from Palm Sunday through the *triduum* to Ascension and Pentecost. Indeed, since the "end" of the Christ narrative is the Parousia, there is a very real sense in which this storyline points toward Advent and the consummation of all things, just as human life always points toward death. This makes the *triduum* and Advent moments into matrices of unfathomable profundity. Nevertheless, one is always at some point in time in that story. Lectionary preachers often comment on the urge to preach Easter in Lent and to preach the cross in Easter. There are times and sermons in which that is the fitting thing to do, but for the most part, the preacher should trust the process of the church year with its unfolding story of grace.

To return to the business of intertwined interpretations, we find in the context of the Christian year another way to "hear" the story of the prodigal. The intention of Lent 4-C clearly stakes its claim in the larger narrative of salvation as the Sunday of reconciliation. But a note of hermeneutical caution is in order. If the preacher takes the prodigal as the way into this theme, he or she will encounter some caution lights and some perhaps unexpected homiletical options precisely because of the vicissitudes of those varied strands of layered interpretation.

In the lectionary the lesson opens by setting the telling of the parable in response to scribal grumbling that Jesus "welcomes and eats" with sinners. To understand this context we must turn to the Lukan setting where we find that this is the third of three parables Luke has Jesus tell in response to the Pharisees who are critical of Jesus' close association with the outcasts of Jewish society. Whether Luke is obliquely criticizing the synagogue of his time for not accepting Christian Gentiles or whether he has in mind Christian criticism of other Christians can only be conjecture. What is clear is that the parables of the lost sheep (Luke 15:3-7), the lost coin (15:8-10), and the prodigal are all interpreted by Luke to make the point that God rejoices more over the repentant sinner than over any other soul. So, for Luke, the heart of reconciliation is repentance, and the prodigal's return is seen as repentance.[1] Surely this Lukan emphasis is one way and in fact the "mainstream" way of understanding the Lenten theme of reconciliation.

But the Lent 4 preacher is not through with the exegesis. From the point of view of a first-century Palestinian, this story might not sound much like a story of repentance, particularly if repentance must include contrition. As the text goes, the younger of two sons, having already sold a quit-claim deed to that portion of his father's farm that would come to him when the patriarch died, has squandered the money and is starving. He is also thoroughly humiliated, having been reduced to trying to eke out sustenance by feeding pigs. He decides to go home and beg for a job as a hired laborer. There is no mention of contrition here; the phrase "he came to himself" seems to imply nothing more than a realistic recognition of his plight. Indeed, his rehearsed speech would probably have been heard by our Palestinian as a slightly cynical "set piece." But however this may be, it turns out to be irrelevant because the father runs to him (an undignified thing for a patriarch to do!) and embraces him before he can get his speech out. Then the father not only calls for a feast and dresses him as a person of honor but puts a ring on his finger. The signet, or sealing-ring, which the lad would have given up when he sold his share of the property, is now replaced, and it sounds for all the world as if he is once again an heir to property.

Here the Palestinian listener might be predictably upset at the injustice of the thing. If the young man had sold the rights to his share and that has been reinvested, what he now claims would have to come from his elder brother's share. Now the listener's sympathies would be very much with this brother, and the father's actions would have appeared grossly unfair. The elder's anger would have been seen as perfectly justified and not small-hearted at all. Then the father consoles his eldest by saying: "all that is mine is yours" (15:31). One must assume that now the Palestinian listener would have been flabbergasted because the father seems to be announcing an absurdity; he has given his younger son land without taking it away from his brother. Thus what we may surmise would be a Palestinian-Jewish take on this parable is indeed about reconciliation, forgiveness, and restoration. But it seems to downplay what Luke and most of the Christian tradition have identified as repentance: acknowledgment, contrition, and amendment. Rather, it seems to suggest that reconciliation is God's doing, and moreover it defies all human calculations of justice and even possibility.

Now of course this too is part of the Christian tradition. It has been part of the proclamation of the gospel from Paul throughout Christian history, exploding periodically now in Tertullian, then in Francis of Assisi, again in Luther, and so forth. The biblical tradition itself carries both of these nuances of the core Christian doctrine of reconciliation.

Thus if we step back and look at the hermeneutic of the narrative cycles of the lectionary we find the following:

1. An overarching plan to tell the whole Christian story of salvation from beginning to end and back to the beginning again, in more or less chronological fashion. This narrative of salvation history, and the ways in which it enables Christians to relive the story of their faith, was the subject of chapter 2.

2. The chronology of the foundational Christian narrative exists together with an emphasis on "themes," which represent developed Christian doctrines. Thus the chronological "story" of Advent and

Christmas presents the Incarnation,[2] the Sundays of Epiphany manifest Jesus' identity as the Christ, and Lent walks us through the process of self-examination, acknowledgment of sin, repentance (including both contrition and penance), reconciliation, and the promise of salvation. In the first half of the year, the lessons are arranged according to the chronological-doctrinal scheme of themes. The lectionary of the church year reads the Bible from a certain perspective. It is a different perspective than would come from reading it, or any of the books in it, *lectio continua*. It is a different perspective than reading it looking for an answer to a question such as "What must I do to be saved?" It is a perspective based on the assumption that living the church year, reading the Christian story, and liturgically inhabiting it year after year will enable one to understand reality more and more in terms of God's will and God's love. It is a perspective that assumes that living this story over and over again "forms" one and the way one sees the world more and more in the mind of Christ. In this perspective the classical Christian doctrines of Incarnation, and so on, emerge from the "themes" of the church year.

3. These themes, however, are not univocal. For instance, the theme of Advent 1 seems clearly to be the Last Judgment and the dreadful things associated with it. But it also holds out hope of good things in the terrible eschatological appearance of God. Thus Advent 1-A reads Isaiah 64:1-9 in which it is prayed that God would "tear open the heavens and come down, so that the mountains would quake at your presence" (64:1) and confesses that "We have all become like one who is unclean, and all our righteous deeds are like a filthy cloth" (64:6a). The passage ends with the plea that God would not remember this iniquity and would consider that "we are all your people" (64:9). This prayer that the Day of the Lord might be a day not only of wrath but of salvation is echoed in the psalm (80:1-7, 16-18) in which God is compared to a shepherd and the psalmist prays "let your face shine, that we may be saved" and in 1 Corinthians 1:3-9 in which Christians are promised that as they wait for the Parousia, "He will also strengthen you to the end, so that you may be blameless on the day of our Lord Jesus Christ" (1:8). Thus the theme of the Second Coming is presented with both its traditional sides. It is a day of terrible judgment and a day of salvation. One must note, however, that salvation is connected on one hand with forgiveness of acknowledged sin (Isaiah) and on the other with perseverance and holiness (1 Corinthians). On this Sunday the Gospel, the centerpiece of the readings, is Mark 13:24-37, the "Little Apocalypse" in which Christians are warned of the

impending time of destruction of the end-time and are exhorted to "keep awake," that is to say, one must suppose, to live every day as though one would be judged for eternity that very evening. Clearly the doctrine of the Last Judgment, particularly if inscribed with such elements as the general resurrection of the dead (or the rejoining of the waiting souls with their bodies, as medieval theology had it), is "thick" enough to occupy year after year of Advent 1 preaching even without further complication.

4. As we have seen in the case of the parables of the good Samaritan and the prodigal, the biblical texts themselves contain the strands of different contexts and understandings. Thus if we return to the Advent 1-A Isaiah lesson, we meet the puzzling passage: "But you were angry, and we sinned; because you hid yourself we transgressed" (64:5b). Here the acknowledgment of human sin seems tempered with a bit of blame-sharing. Surely without the presence of God's grace, humans cannot but sin. But here we meet the conundrums of "election" and "theodicy" with which Christian theologians since Augustine have struggled. Do we lack of God's grace because we turn away and refuse, or is it somehow because God has withdrawn the Divine Presence from us? Taken in its fullness, human experience seems to provide for both. At times we cannot but know our world as God-forsaken and our wills as in bondage. At other times, we sense that our plight is self-inflicted, that we turn away and refuse love, preferring anger and bitterness. It is neither simply one nor the other. The first lesson of Advent 1-A offers the preacher the possibility of dealing with this human existentiality under the proper theme of judgment.

Thus we can view the hermeneutic of the lectionary as fourfold. The immediate aim is to retell the "story" of salvation year by year so that the Christian can relive the foundational events of the faith. Intertwined with this is the thematic presentation of those basic Christian doctrines that have crystallized from the story. Implicit in this presentation of doctrinal themes is the richness and depth of the doctrines themselves. Thus to preach the idea that God became human, that God took on human nature in order that human nature might become divinized, is a daunting but important task for a preacher. Indeed, in exploring this one doctrinal aspect of the Incarnation, one encounters such questions as the place of Mary and her human "yes" to God's approach to her and the implied question of our "yes" to God's approaches to us.

And finally, the lectionary exegete encounters the stubborn otherness of the biblical texts themselves. One of the criticisms leveled at the church year by Reformed theologians in the sixteenth and seventeenth centuries was that it impeded direct access to Scripture. In part that was because of the late medieval dismissal of the sanctoral cycle, but in part it was because the "thematic" hermeneutic inherent in the church year lectionary can move the preacher very quickly away from an encounter with Scripture itself to an exposition of doctrine. Lectionary texts often fit wonderfully with the doctrinal themes of their particular Sundays, but they also often contain material that seems to rub up against doctrine. This is the stuff of the human situation and the Divine Mystery, which doctrine, even with all its subtlety, sometimes seems to try to explain or reconcile with too much facility. One of the graces of the lectionary is that the themes of the narrative Sundays provide a framework within which to explore the doctrinal and biblical nuances and paradoxes, Sunday by Sunday, without losing one's way or losing track of one's pastoral commitment to preach the Gospel with and to the people of God gathered for worship.

It is to some of these contemporary issues and values of the lectionary that we now turn.

CHAPTER FOUR

PREACHING THE
LECTIONARY TODAY

In this chapter we turn to the ways in which preaching the lectionary enriches and deepens the preaching life and ministry of the church. We must begin by recognizing that because of the demands of time and schedule, preachers often live from sermon to sermon, without the breathing room to think about the cumulative effect of preaching. The weekly task of sermon preparation can become so consuming that the preacher's definition of preaching can shrink to include only what is required for each worship service. The preacher can lose contact with a broader vision of a preaching ministry, of the theological and pastoral work that the ongoing ministry of preaching can accomplish in the life of the contemporary church. Lectionary preaching in general, and the *Revised Common Lectionary* in particular, provides a lens for thinking about preaching more broadly as an ongoing ministry and not only as a weekly task.

Yet not all preachers will read from the same perspective the material about the liturgical year and the lectionary that is found in chapters 2 and 3. Preachers whose worship life is formed and experienced in a highly liturgical church, like Catholicism, Anglicanism, or Lutheranism, will recognize instinctively the rhythms of the liturgical year to which those chapters draw attention, even if they are unable to name and describe them as explicitly as those chapters do. Preachers in a liturgical tradition in which the Eucharist is celebrated weekly know by formation and practice that each Sunday enacts and proclaims the life, death, and resurrection of Jesus Christ and that each Sunday's celebration and enactment of the Jesus story is matched by the annual cycle of living the Jesus story throughout the liturgical year.

For many Protestant preachers, whose traditions historically have placed the preached word at the center of corporate worship, the material in chapters 2 and 3 reads somewhat differently. For traditions in which the proclamation of the Word of God as known in the biblical text is at the center of worship, the lectionary is most regularly understood as a teaching vehicle for bringing the Bible more fully into the worship service rather than as a liturgical entity in its own right. For these traditions, living the rhythms of the liturgical year is often something to be learned rather than an organic part of their corporate worship life. These preachers and their traditions are shaped more by a sense of the whole sweep of the biblical story than by the liturgical reenactment of the life and death of Christ.[1]

The genius of the *Revised Common Lectionary* is that it attempts to accommodate both perspectives. The rhythms of the liturgical year and the sweep of the larger biblical story are present in its selection of passages. As noted in the introduction, this book also attempts to bridge these two perspectives in its coauthorship by writers whose liturgical and preaching formation is in each of the two perspectives: one author is an Anglican priest, the other a clergy in a Reformed tradition. The two authors do not articulate or understand the role and place of the lectionary in the preaching and worship life of the church in exactly the same way because of their different formation and church experiences. Yet in drawing on both perspectives to write this book, the theological and pastoral common denominator is the lectionary and its gift to the preaching ministry of the church in all its varieties.

This chapter will identify and discuss three contributions that lectionary preaching makes to the ministry and life of the church: a reclaimed relationship of time and story, a lived experience of each congregation as part of the body of Christ, and a fresh perspective on pastoral authority and congregational identity.

Preaching in the Church's Time

Story and Time

The history of the development of the liturgical year and the lectionary (outlined in chapters 1 and 2) shows that from its earliest days, the church understood that there is an inseparable relationship between story and time. As those chapters note, the early liturgies, and especially the creation of the liturgy around the events of Holy Week, were a mimetic "reliving" of the foundational events of the church's life made necessary by the passage of time. If those events remained bound to one limited moment in the past, each successive generation would become completely reliant on someone else's reporting about the foundational events of the faith with no way to experience those events for itself.

From the very beginning of the development of their corporate religious life, both Judaism and Christianity found ways in which particular moments in history could become repeated and repeatable moments in the experience of successive generations of believers. Religious experience is not limited to the relatively few people who participated in the events remembered in the stories of the Exodus or the events at the end of Jesus' life. The reenactment of the story of the exodus in the feast of Passover, for example, or the events of Jesus' last days in the celebration of Holy Week redefine how a worshiping community keeps time. Through the intersection of religious story and time, past, present, and future are now always available in the corporate life of the community. Timekeeping is not simply about the passage of minutes, days, or weeks. The way we keep time also tells us a story about how we structure our world and locate ourselves in it.

The timekeeping of the church is structured around the story of Jesus' life, death, and resurrection. In the United States, however, there are two major cultural cycles of time that govern how people mark the flow of the year. This chapter was written right before the Memorial Day holiday, the three-day weekend that marks the unofficial beginning of the summer season. Memorial Day weekend is balanced by the three-day Labor Day weekend, which marks the official ending of the summer season. For most U.S. citizens, these two holidays that bracket the summer season determine the flow and movement of time, since they closely parallel the end points of the school year. Neither holiday was created as a seasonal marker. Memorial Day commemorates war dead, and Labor Day celebrates the contributions of the labor force, yet these intentions are subsumed into the holidays' seasonal functions. The yearly routine begins at Labor Day and ends at Memorial Day—and in between, there is summer. Even individuals and families without school-age children live according to these temporal rhythms, because the school year/summer pattern is wholly integrated into the general U.S. lifestyle.

This well-known way of keeping time carries its own story with it, although most U.S. citizens do not reflect intentionally on this story. The Memorial Day/Labor Day calculation is not simply about the arrival of summer, since according to the solar calendar, the first day of summer arrives on June 21, almost a full month after Memorial Day kicks off the summer season. The story of Memorial Day/Labor Day is the story of work and leisure but also of prosperity, economic class, and the wealth to take a vacation. The hourly wage earner and the corporate CEO do not enter the Memorial Day/Labor Day story at the same point, nor might they recognize it as the same story. A week at a rented cabin in a state park and a month-long sojourn at one's own (second) home at the ocean tell different stories about work and leisure.

The second cycle is even more explicitly calendrical because this cycle calculates time from January 1 to December 31 of each given year. The end of one calendar year and the beginning of the next is always met with great anticipation. To be home alone on New Year's Eve is a social embarrassment to many people, when in reality, December 31 is not all that different from December 30 or January 2.

The story that accompanies this reckoning of time is a story of endings and beginnings, of chance and intentionality. New Year's resolutions suggest that we can control our destiny, whereas New Year's Eve champagne toasts and the eating of foods that bring good luck on New Year's Day suggest that serendipity may be the stronger power. This reckoning of time, too, tells an economic and commercial story because the most lasting significance of this calendrical cycle is as a fiscal year and the time period on which income tax is calculated. The passage of time and one's financial worth are closely linked in the January 1/December 31 story.

These two temporal cycles exercise great pull on the life of the church in the United States, yet neither of these cycles keeps time in a way that reflects the stories and rhythms of the Christian life. For Christians, the beginning of a new year is neither January 1 nor the beginning of the new school year, but is the start of Advent, when the church renews its anticipation and hope for the coming of the Lord. The church year ends neither with New Year's Eve nor with Memorial Day, but with the eschatological expectation of Christ the King Sunday, which announces that Jesus is sovereign over the church. The lectionary enacts a different calendar and so challenges the dominant stories and ways of telling time in the United States.

Congregations struggle to allow the church's calendar to be the shaping calendar for their corporate life. It is a rare U.S. church, liturgically based or otherwise, that does not switch to its summer worship schedule after Memorial Day weekend, regardless of where Memorial Day comes within the liturgical year. The festival of Pentecost often falls after Memorial Day, so that the celebration of one of the main festivals of the church year is dictated by the vagaries of summer vacations and summer schedules. More importantly, the storytelling and timekeeping of the Memorial Day/Labor Day cycle cuts short the storytelling and timekeeping of the liturgical cycle. The story of vacation and leisure is privileged over the story of the gift of the Holy Spirit and the birth of the church.

When one preaches according to the texts assigned in the *Revised Common Lectionary*, preacher and congregation are drawn into the church's timekeeping. The markers of time in the church's calendar are the seasons of Advent, Christmas, Lent, Easter, and Pentecost. To live according to the calendar of the liturgical year is to live as if something other than summer vacation or the end of a 365-day period determines the rhythm of one's life. By virtue of preaching from the lectionary and keeping the church's time, the lectionary preacher challenges the storytelling and timekeeping of the dominant U.S. culture even before an individual sermon is preached on any given Sunday. Stories of individual achievement, personal success, and national pride are countered by the story of the life and death of Jesus that transforms time.

Three specific examples from lessons of the RCL demonstrate how keeping time with the church's story can reframe a community's life. New Year's Eve and New Year's Day fall within the Christmas season in the liturgical year. While the dominant U.S. culture is celebrating the arrival of a new year on those days, the church continues to celebrate the arrival of God-with-us, the Christ child, who is at the heart of the Christmas season. The story the church tells on December 31 and January 1 is not individual resolutions and the bottom line of taxable income, but of the Christmas joy that makes all things possible. New possibility comes not from resolve or good luck, but from the renewed presence of God in the world. December 31 and January 1 are in the middle of the Christmas season, not the beginning of a new season.

Christmas is the shortest season in the liturgical year, and we risk making it even shorter when we reckon time according to New Year's Day.[2] The lessons for the First Sunday after Christmas in all three years continue the Christmas story. In Year A, for example, the Gospel lesson

(Matt 2:13-23) tells the story of the flight to Egypt and the slaughter of the innocents, stories that highlight the risk that God-with-us poses to the dominant culture. To pass over that lesson in order to follow the January 1/December 31 cycle is to contradict the very message of the text by choosing to follow the story of the dominant culture instead of the Jesus story.

The second example comes from Ordinary Time. As was discussed in chapter 3, the lessons in Ordinary Time, Old Testament, Epistle, and Gospel, are each selected according to a pattern of semi-continuous readings.[3] As the church moves through summer and fall, the Ordinary Time lessons provide the broadest sweep of the biblical story of any season in the church year.

For U.S. citizens, the Memorial Day/Labor Day cycle is punctuated by the Fourth of July, the holiday that commemorates the creation of the United States as an independent nation, free from British sovereignty. The Fourth of July's date remains fixed (that is, unlike Memorial Day, which has been moved from May 30 to the last Monday in May), so the Fourth of July can fall on a Sunday. A Fourth of July sermon presents the preacher with an interesting dilemma and raises questions of the merging of religion and nationalism and how the stories of the dominant culture and of the church will be given voice.

The lessons from Ordinary Time, Year B appointed for the Sunday that falls between July 3 and 9 inclusive are amazingly suggestive of ways to negotiate the overlap of these two often competing stories. The OT lesson is 2 Samuel 5:1-10, the story of David becoming king of all Israel and Judah. The story includes its own cautionary notes about the exercise of power. The inhabitants of Jerusalem mocked David, saying that even the blind and the lame would turn him back (2 Sam 5:5), but David's conquest of Jerusalem was successful. The aftermath of David's conquest was that the blind and lame were expelled from Jerusalem (2 Sam 5:8) and David named the city after himself (2 Sam 5:9). David is triumphant (2 Sam 5:10), but the Bible does not hesitate to show the dark sides of success and nationalistic power.

The Gospel lesson for Year B also challenges the preacher to preach in the church's time and not according to the expectations of the national calendar. The gospel lesson is Mark 6:14-29, the death of John the Baptist at the hand of King Herod. This story, in even more detail than the lesson from 2 Samuel, paints a picture of the caprice of power and the abuses to which that caprice can lead.

Both of these lessons provide a powerful starting point for a Fourth of July sermon, but only if the preacher is willing to listen first to the time and story of the church and then turn to the time and story of the nation. If one begins with the assumptions of the national story and time, the good news that the church's story can bring on this day may be lost.

The third example suggests a slightly different aspect of the theological reframing of story and time that the lectionary can accomplish. Contemporary lectionaries are constructed on a three-year cycle, so that the same texts recur as the basis for preaching every three years. The repetition of the lectionary cycles contains within it an important theological and pastoral affirmation—that the texts of the Bible and the stories of the church take on new significance each time they are preached.

If the meaning of the texts and the stories were simply fixed in time, each Christian would be allotted one Christmas sermon and one Easter sermon for a lifetime. The proclamation of the good news could be accomplished simply by rereading that same sermon each Christmas and Easter throughout one's lifetime. This is not how the good news is proclaimed, however. The texts of the Bible move with us as we progress through life. The way one hears and receives the good news at twenty-one and the way one hears and receives the good news at sixty are not the same, even though the words of the biblical text do not change.

The repetition of the lectionary enables each passage of human life to be set within the larger Christian story. The Gospel lesson for the Fourth Sunday of Advent, Year B, Luke 1:26-38, illustrates this well. This lesson recounts the story of the annunciation of the birth of Jesus to Mary by the angel Gabriel. This story is well-known and well-loved from Christmas pageant and song, yet its meaning is not as straightforward as its pageant appropriations may suggest. One's own personal timekeeping can overlap with the church's timekeeping in surprising and powerful ways.

The young teenage girl in the congregation has heard the story of the annunciation her whole life; she may even have played Mary or the angel Gabriel in the Christmas pageant. Yet the first time she hears the story after learning about sex and "where babies come from," she listens to the lesson with renewed interest and curiosity. The woman who is six months pregnant with her third child hears the good news of this lesson in a very different way from the woman who, after years of expensive infertility treatments, has come to accept the painful truth that she will never conceive a child. This woman once saw herself in Mary, but now listens for "nothing will be impossible with God" (Luke 1:37) as a promise of something else.

The repetition of the lectionary allows the church's story to be available at all the moments of a human life. Worshipers are able to place their own story and time into the cycle of the church's story and time.

Continuity through Time

In addition to highlighting the interrelationship of story and time, preaching the lectionary makes another broad contribution to the way time is experienced by a worshiping congregation. The liturgical year assumes that all fifty-two weeks of the calendar year belong to the continuum of the church story. No weeks or months are bracketed as being outside the Christian story. The very existence of Ordinary Time as a liturgical marker underscores this point, since not all of the church's life is lived in the narrative seasons of Advent, Christmas, Lent, and Easter. The liturgical time outside of those seasons reminds the church that the daily Christian existence is holy too and belongs to the ongoing story of how one lives out one's baptism.

As a result, no Sunday in the liturgical year exists as an isolated Sunday, but is always held in relationship with the Sundays that surround it. The lectionary names the four Sundays of Advent, Christmas Day and the First Sunday after Christmas Day, and Epiphany and the numbered Sundays after the Epiphany. The season of Lent is identified by the First through Sixth Sundays in Lent, with each day of Holy Week explicitly named. Easter Sunday is followed by the Second through Seventh Sundays of Easter. The interrelationship of the Sundays in Ordinary Time between Trinity Sunday and Christ the King Sunday is communicated by the semi-continuous readings that constitute the lessons.[4]

The interconnectedness of this way of keeping and marking time is formative for the life of a congregation. It is a weekly reminder that Christian life is not calculated according to individual Sundays, but according to the broader sweep of time in which each successive Sunday plays a part. When church bulletins identify a Sunday by its place in the liturgical year, they remind congregations of the calendar according to which they are called to live their lives. If each Sunday has its own distinctive place in the worship life of a congregation, not all Sundays are the same. Church attendance marks one's participation in the church's time and story, and to miss a Sunday is to miss part of the ongoing story. The lectionary's enactment of the continuity of the church's story through time can pull people away from sporadic attendance at worship because worship is not defined by individual Sunday services. Rather, the weekly contin-uum of worship takes on theological and pastoral significance as the locus of the presence of God and the carrier of the church's story.

An awareness of the continuity of the church's story through and across time can also inform the way the preacher approaches sermon preparation and preaching. If one preaches in the context of a fifty-two-week, theologically and liturgically interconnected year, by necessity one begins to think about preaching as something other than a succession of individual sermons. In the context of the lectionary, a preaching ministry becomes a *continuum* of sermons rather than a *succession* of sermons in which each week's sermon stands alone.

The sense of the continuity of time that the lectionary offers a wor-shiping congregation also can widen the preacher's narrow focus in sermon preparation on what one will preach on any given Sunday. Because the lectionary regularly rehearses the story of faith, the preacher can free him-self or herself from the often self-imposed pressure to preach the totality of the Christian story in each and every sermon. One can trust the story of the faith to be present and available. Sermon preparation can begin with the knowledge that preacher and congregation enter into an ongoing story each Sunday. That story does not have to be created anew week after week because one is always preaching the church's story. The shape that the story of faith takes for people's lives changes from week to week, and from congregation to congregation, depending on the lessons for the day and the circumstances in church and world. The number and types of sermons that the lectionary can generate are limitless, and because of the lec-tionary context, the preacher is able to think about each Sunday's sermon as part of a preaching ministry that moves across and through time.

Members of the Body of Christ

As was outlined briefly in chapter 1, the liturgical reforms of Vatican II generated a new lectionary for Catholics, the *Ordo Lectionum Missae* (1969). Protestant churches in North America were especially interested in these reforms, and in the 1970s many denominations adapted the *Ordo Lectionum Missae* for their own settings.[5] The desire in North America to create a common lectionary that Protestants could share led to the formation of the Consultation on Common Texts.[6] This ecumenical group worked with the many lectionaries that were in use among Catholics and Protestants, and in 1983 the Consultation on Common Texts produced the forerunner of the RCL, the *Common Lectionary*. The production of this lectionary was a landmark in ecumenical relations. The first years in which the CL was in use served as a trial period to identify the strengths and weaknesses of the lectionary (see discussion in chapter 1). In 1992, as a result of this trial period, the *Revised Common Lectionary* was published.[7] The RCL remains the main ecumenical lectionary in use in North America and many countries around the world.[8]

The very existence of the RCL is testimony to the possibilities of ecumenism and the interconnectedness of different Christian communions. Its beginnings derive from ecumenical instincts and desires, and the enactment of this ecumenical desire through its usage Sunday after Sunday remains one of the essential contributions of the RCL to the life of the Christian church. The ecumenical significance of the RCL can perhaps be summarized most helpfully around two themes: the enactment of Christian unity and the formation of a communal ecclesiology.

Christian Unity

The readings of the RCL provide a model of Christian unity that is able to rise above the many issues of doctrine and practice that divide ecclesiastical communions from one another in the contemporary world. Churches that cannot agree on who can be ordained, what is proper baptismal practice, who can celebrate and receive at the eucharistic table, or how one defines sin can share in the same lessons Sunday after Sunday. The lessons of the RCL, especially the Gospel lessons, are so similar to the *Ordo* as well that when they are read in worship, one actually catches a glimpse of the church universal to which the creeds point and in which the prayers of the faithful place their hope. Each congregation and communion that uses the three-year lectionary cycle is committed to sharing in the same scriptural stories and living in the same liturgical time Sunday by Sunday with other congregations and communions.

This unity can be experienced in small and large ways by individual Christians and congregations. For the individual worshiper, it is simultaneously humbling and enlivening to sit in Sunday morning worship and know that the lessons one is hearing read are also being heard by millions of worshipers in churches across North America and, in many instances, the world. To know that one's relative or friend, separated by distance and perhaps by denomination or communion, is sharing the same lessons on Sunday morning is to experience in miniature the promise and joy of one universal church. The shared lessons are a tangible reminder of the faith stories and traditions that predate divisions within the church.

For congregations, the shared lessons underscore points of unity with congregations across the street or across town. Even something as mundane as the religion pages in the Saturday newspaper become a pointer to Christian unity. By reading the church announcements, one can notice which congregations are using the lectionary texts, as well as the ways in which sermon titles and topics compare and contrast across these congregations.

For clergy, the lectionary provides the occasion for ecumenical gatherings around the shared pastoral responsibility of preaching these lessons. Each clergy participant in an ecumenical lectionary conversation comes to the lessons from his or her own denominational and confessional perspective, and all these perspectives are refracted together around the biblical texts themselves. Lectionary study groups have immediate benefits for clergy on the most pragmatic level, since the individual preacher is able to draw on the resources provided by a community of preachers in his or her own sermon preparation. These conversations have theological and ecumenical importance as well. When a variety of perspectives gather together around the scriptural traditions that they hold in common, preachers begin to recognize what their tradition brings to the ecumenical conversation and what they can learn from the traditions of others.

The three-year lectionary stands as a sign of the possibilities of genuine unity that still elude the broken Christian church. This is not to suggest that lectionary use is the answer to all the problems that continue to plague ecumenical efforts. Lectionary use in and of itself will not lead seamlessly to recognition of orders of ordination from one communion to another nor to complete unity at the eucharistic table. Yet lectionary use in Sunday worship is one of the most visible and hopeful ecumenical acts that a local congregation or denomination can practice. It points beyond denominational and confessional identity and acknowledges the shared traditions of a greater Christian whole.

Communal Ecclesiology

Lectionary use helps congregations understand themselves as more than simply isolated entities. This is related to the question of church unity, but is not identical with it. The hope of ecumenism is the fulfill-ment of the eschatological promise of one united church. A communal ecclesiology highlights the awareness that a congregation is defined and shaped by more than its particular present moment in time and place. Paul's metaphor of the body of Christ (1 Cor 12) pertains as clearly to congregations as it does to individual believers. To be the church at the corner of 12th and Pine is the beginning point for ecclesiology, not the end point.

For most Christians, the experience of church is intensely local—one's ecclesial identity is defined by the congregation of which one is a mem-ber. Local participation is essential because through it one experiences the particulars and details of the Christian life. Christianity is made incarnate in one's local religious community. There is also a downside to the local, however, especially in contemporary U.S. culture that puts a premium on individual achievement, freedom, success, and autonomy. In this cultural context, it can be difficult to look beyond one's own congre-gation. Each individual congregation may operate out of its own ecclesi-ology, its own sense of what it means to be church, but that ecclesiology does not often contain an explicit affirmation of the church universal as part of the congregation's identity. Church mission statements, for exam-ple, may communicate a sense of what one will experience inside the doors of a particular church building, but they rarely make prominent that an individual church is in actuality only one member of the body of Christ.

Preaching the lectionary can move congregations to place their local experience in a broader context of what it means to be church. As noted above, the practice of sharing Sunday scripture lessons with churches around North America and the globe points to an expansive definition of church. The stories and traditions that shape Sunday morning worship are not simply the prerogative of an individual congregation and pastor. This recognition can seem foreign and even frightening to many Protestant congregations, especially those with congregational-based polities and who define themselves in terms of freedom of the pulpit. But freedom of the pulpit is often not a genuine theological or pastoral good but simply a reflection of the individualism and subjectivity of the preacher.

Regardless of denominational background and self-presentation, no congregation exists in isolation from other congregations and ecclesial communities. A congregation's identity is shaped by its local culture and mission and also by its place in the broader Christian community. To use the lectionary is to acknowledge that one is in partnership with traditions of the church that are not simply of one's own devising. Each and every congregation is part of a story and tradition larger than itself, and the use of the lectionary for preaching helps to make those ties visible and explicit in the weekly worship of the congregation.

Since the three-year lectionary cycle evolved from the ancient lectionaries of the church, the lectionary lessons also broaden the notion of church by locating each congregation in a continuum with communities and congregations through time. As was discussed in chapter 2, many of the practices and lessons that mark Holy Week and Easter today can be traced back to the fourth century C.E. The three-year lectionary cycle gives each congregation a weekly experience of the "great . . . cloud of witnesses" of Hebrews 12:1. To share in the readings of the lectionary is not only to participate in the ecumenical movement of the current day. It is also to place oneself in the living history of worshipers whose faith and practices have been formed by these texts through the centuries.

Pastoral Authority and Identity

The third contribution of lectionary preaching to the preaching ministry of the church is the fresh perspective it offers on pastoral authority and identity.

The RCL provides a fixed schedule of lessons for the church year, yet there is still tremendous freedom of choice for the preacher who uses the lectionary. Each week provides three lessons and a psalm, any of which can speak to the preaching needs and desires of a congregation. Given those multiple lessons, text selection for a lectionary preacher is the same as it is for non-lectionary preachers: one listens for the intersection between the biblical texts and the life of one's congregation and the world. The lectionary preacher does not lose his or her autonomy with regard to preaching because the multiple lessons provide the lectionary preacher with a range of options. Yet when a preacher is guided by the lectionary for text selection, the preacher acknowledges week after week that his or her preaching participates in the ongoing Christian story that has shaped Christian preaching since its first centuries. Since preaching decisions are to some degree governed by that story, there is a subtle shift in the way the preacher's authority is configured.

In this context, the preacher's authority ultimately comes from the recognition that his or her preaching ministry shares in a story that predates any individual ministry and that will continue long after any one preacher retires. The preacher's authority is not determined solely by personal charisma, or by the authority with which an individual congregation invests its preacher. The lectionary preacher shares in a ministry that depends first on the power and presence of the preached word of God, not the power and presence of the individual preacher.

Lectionary use makes explicit that the authority for a preaching ministry involves more than any one preacher's weekly preaching, regardless of a preacher's gifts. Each preacher's authority to preach also involves the "cloud of witnesses" of preachers who have preached before and who preach alongside him or her. The lectionary preacher locates himself or herself within the church's preaching ministry that stretches through time and place. The texts for Lent, Year A, for example, were in use in the fourth century, and so when the contemporary preacher preaches these texts, he or she adds a fresh sermon to that chorus of sermons on these texts that has resounded through the ages.

To participate in a preaching ministry is to share in one of the oldest theological and pastoral practices of the church. The very act of participation defines the preacher's authority. This can be simultaneously challenging and liberating for the preacher because awareness of the continuum of the church's story becomes one's responsibility as well as the needs of the present moment. Yet the continuum of the church's story and preaching also provides the support and sustenance that empower each preacher to claim his or her authority as a preacher.

The use of the lectionary to govern text selection can remove much of the mystery for the laity about how the preacher selects texts for preaching. The selection of texts for Sunday worship no longer rests completely in the hands of the preacher, where it can often seem to laity like a hidden exercise of power and individual pastoral authority. Instead, the selection of texts for Sunday worship rests in the story and shared practices of the worshiping Christian communion, and laity and clergy alike have equal access to that story and those practices. If a congregation worships according to the lectionary, then the surprise element of "What is the sermon text for this week?" almost completely disappears. With the use of the lectionary, the selection of texts for Sunday morning worship becomes a more public act.

This has important practical and pastoral implications for the relationship between pastor and congregation. The public nature of text selection opens fresh options for worship, congregational educational programs, and Bible study. Because lectionary use enables laity to know in advance the source of each week's readings, lectionary use encourages laity to participate more actively in corporate worship. Sunday's scripture lessons have a context in the ongoing life and story of the church, and laity can share in that story and its enactment in worship through their own engagement with the biblical texts. Adult education programs and Bible study curricula have been built around the lectionary. These programs can increase a congregation's sense that laity and clergy speak the same biblical language and share in the same traditions.

Lectionary-based study programs also bring the laity into a different relationship with the preaching ministry of the church. Because laity can know in advance the texts on which a preacher will preach, they approach each Sunday's sermon with a higher level of expectation and an increased sense of ownership. Sunday's texts are not simply the preacher's texts; they are the church's texts. Lectionary use makes visible the truth that a preacher preaches *for* a congregation, not *to* or *at* a congregation. A congregation has thoughts and hopes about any Sunday's texts, and it is the preacher's responsibility and privilege to give voice to those hopes.

Perhaps most important, because the lectionary gives all participants in worship the same access to each Sunday's biblical texts, the relationship between clergy and laity is equalized to some degree. This shift in relationship is inseparably related to the two contributions of the lectionary discussed earlier in the chapter: the relationship of story and time and the sense of membership in the body of Christ. To shape one's preaching around the interrelationship of story and time inevitably redefines how the preacher understands and experiences the source of authority for preaching and how laity understand their own place in the church's ministry and story. To experience weekly preaching and worship as a practice through which one regularly participates in the body of Christ also redefines the relationship of preacher and congregation.

The presence and continuity of the church's story in the texts that are read across the liturgical year create a shared identity of preacher and congregation. Both come to know their lives and faith as belonging to the church's ongoing story in which they live and move and have their being.

CHAPTER FIVE

PREACHING THE INCARNATIONAL CYCLE

In preceding chapters we have looked at the history of the formation of the church year and the way in which the lectionary principle developed as part of that history. We saw that a fundamental need driving the development of both was the formation of an accessible Christian hermeneutic based on the liturgical reliving of the foundational events of the Christian story, at the center of which was the narrative of Jesus Christ and the Holy Spirit. We also saw that as Christians interacted with their story certain "themes" developed and doctrines crystallized from those themes as Christians pondered them and attempted to integrate them with the ways in which they ordinarily made sense of things.

These theological and doctrinal reflections are evident in the selection of texts for key seasons of the church year. On the first Sunday after Christmas, in Years A, B, and C, when the Prologue to John proclaims the Incarnation of the Divine Word, the Epistle to the Galatians tells us that "God sent his Son, born of a woman . . . so that we might receive adoption," so that we are now children of God and heirs (Gal 4:4). So also, on Palm Sunday when the long Passion Narratives are read, the Epistle proclaims in the words of the great Philippians' hymn that though Christ was in the "form" (or nature) of God, he nevertheless emptied himself and being found in human nature humbled himself to death and that therefore God exalted him as Lord (Phil

2:5-11). And so also at the great Easter Vigil, the traditional time of baptizing from at least the early third century on, Romans explains that all the baptized are baptized into Christ's death so that we will certainly "be united with him in a resurrection like his" (Rom 6:5).

Inherent in the logic of the lectionary is an intertwining of the narrative of God's way with his people and themes that lead to or imply doctrines. At the same time, the church year seems always to have resisted observing doctrines as such. Thus the only Sunday devoted to a doctrine is Trinity Sunday, the Sunday after Pentecost. This was adapted only in the fourteenth century and is usually explained as a way of putting an exclamation point at the end of the narrative cycles of Jesus and the Holy Spirit. It can also be understood as a liturgical marking of the reality of the mystery of the inner life of the Trinity, the mystery that the One God is a relationship.

It is the pastoral and catechetical task of the preacher to open up the narrative of the church year so that all may grow in their ability to see the world through ever deepening and widening Christian lenses, that we "must grow up in every way into him who is the head" (Eph 4:15). Sunday by Sunday the lectionary preacher will help his or her people recognize where they are in the story of salvation, so that they may claim again and again the history and the promise of the people of God as their own.

Part of this will be helping people "get inside" the crucial Christian doctrines that the Christian story implies, such as the Atonement in connection with the *triduum* and the Incarnation in connection with Christmas. But another part is to honor the particularity and integrity of each biblical text. This means paying attention to nuances, paradoxes, and even apparent incongruities, for it is in such "stumbling blocks" to a seamless lectionary narration that the profound "foolishness of the Gospel" is often revealed.

Charting the Season

What is needed first of all is a way for the preacher to have an overview of the trajectory of that part of the narrative to which she or he is attending and then to focus on particular Sundays and on their individual texts. Clearly, there is no single right way to do this, and every preacher will have his or her own preferences. This book will offer one option for proceeding with the task of holding the big picture of a season together with the particularities of each Sunday and its readings. It is a four-step procedure that is aimed at carefully reading all the texts offered and finding threads of continuity as well as moments of creative discontinuity woven into the fabric of the lectionary.

The first step is a chart that the exegete makes sometime before the beginning of a season. The example we will work with in this chapter is Advent, Year C. You will notice that the chart is arranged simply with the Sundays of Advent in a vertical column and the four readings for each Sunday set up horizontally. The lines drawn between them then provide a "box" for each reading for each Sunday. The idea is to read through all the texts for each Sunday in the season at one or two sittings and jot down notes about each text as they are read. These notes are not to be researched or explored in depth. They are first impressions; the object is to get an overall view of the section of the lectionary in question. Indeed, many find this process works best when done in a group setting. That might mean sitting down with church staff or with a clergy group or with a group of interested laypeople to read through the lectionary texts and simply note which ideas pop out in them. When done as a group exercise, a chalkboard or newsprint divided in the same way as the chart can be put up and one person nominated to write down the ideas that emerge. If one is doing this alone, most people will find the exercise most easily accomplished with a legal pad and either colored pencils or highlighters.

When this is completed, the second step is to read over the chart as it now stands and begin to note leading ideas or themes as they appear text by text, Sunday by Sunday. At the same time, one should make note of any apparent incongruities that this or that text may present. In the third step, the preacher reads through the chart again, noting the ways in which the identified themes may or may not relate to each other or form a kind of process, such as the one we noted in chapter 3 in moving through Lent. In that case the movement was from self-examination and acknowledgment of sin through reconciliation to the promise of new life.

After these three steps are completed, the preacher is familiar enough with all the lessons of the season to begin to sketch out sermon "proposals" to himself or herself for each of the Sundays in that portion of the church year under study. This move from texts to sermon is the fourth step of the process. This chapter will model one way of moving from text to sermon through the use of sermon "platforms." These platforms should be completed for all Sundays of the liturgical cycle before proceeding to write individual sermons. In this way, the liturgical year is the context for all the work of sermon creation.

We will begin our charting experiment with the Sunday before Advent (the last Sunday of Ordinary Time, often called "Reign of Christ" Sunday), since the theme of Christ's sovereignty "sets the table" for Advent. Since our case study for Advent will be Year C, the Sunday preceding Advent C is in Year B. Because Advent points toward Christmas, and as a season of waiting is pregnant with Christmas themes, we must also include the lessons for the first part of the Christmas season in our charting in order to tell the entire story of the incarnational cycle.

Step One: First Impressions

After identifying the lessons for the last Sunday in Ordinary Time, "Reign of Christ Sunday," Year B, we are ready to begin step one. The first reading for that Sunday is 2 Samuel 23:1-7:

> Now these are the last words of David:
> The oracle of David, son of Jesse,
>   the oracle of the man whom God exalted,
> the anointed of the God of Jacob,
>   the favorite of the Strong One of Israel:
> The spirit of the LORD speaks through me,
>   his word is upon my tongue.
> The God of Israel has spoken,
>   the Rock of Israel has said to me:
> One who rules over people justly,
>   ruling in the fear of God,
> is like the light of morning,
>   like the sun rising on a cloudless morning,
>   gleaming from the rain on the grassy land.
> Is not my house like this with God?
>   For he has made with me an everlasting covenant,
>   ordered in all things and secure.
> Will he not cause to prosper
>   all my help and my desire?
> But the godless are all like thorns that are thrown away;
>   for they cannot be picked up with the hand;
> to touch them one uses an iron bar
>   or the shaft of a spear.
>   And they are entirely consumed in fire on the spot.

Among the things that jump out immediately at the reader are that "these are the last words of David," as well as the clear way in which David identifies himself as the chosen, favored, anointed one (king) who has God's spirit. Based on David's just governance, God has made an everlasting covenant with David and with David's "house," or descendants. That just governance is beautiful, but it has another side: the "godless" are rejected and are to be destroyed "in fire on the spot."

Obviously, the preceding paragraph is just a kind of synopsis of this lesson. As we enter this synopsis in the first box of our chart, in this case, in non-boldfaced type, we have the first half of the first box in our chart for Reign of Christ Sunday. We would then proceed to do the same thing for the second and third readings and for the Gospel. At this point, the chart for this Sunday is half done (see below). One would then proceed to do the same thing for all four Sundays of Advent and for Christmas Eve, Christmas, and the First Sunday after Christmas.

Step One of Exegetical Chart for the Last Sunday before Advent
Reign of Christ Sunday: Year B

Lesson 1	Lesson 2	Lesson 3	Gospel
2 Sam 23:1-7:	Ps 132:1-13 (14-19):	Rev 1:4b-8:	John 18:33-37:
Last words of David. Davidic kingship-line. The Spirit of God speaks through King David. A just ruler pleases God. Everlasting covenant with David. Destruction of the "godless."	Song of Davidic history with God. Ark and God's presence. The LORD's oath to David: "A son, the fruit of your body I will set upon your throne." God's promise to establish Zion and David's line.	Grace and peace from him who is, was, and is to come and from Christ, first born from the dead and ruler of the kings of the earth. He made us kingdom and priests serving his God and Father.	Jesus before Pilate. Are you King of the Jews? My kingdom is not from this world. So you are a king? You say so . . . I was born, came into this world to testify to the truth.

Step Two: Identification of Themes

The second step is to identify themes. In our chart, these appear in **boldface type**. Themes emerge from the text as understood in the light of other things we know, from the other texts of this Sunday, from the charted synopses of the lessons of Advent and Christmas, from our intuitions about the church year, and from our general store of theological knowledge. Thus we are aware that Jesus is descended from the line of David, and we see that this seems to be alluded to in the psalm for the last Sunday of Ordinary Time, Year B: "A son, the fruit of your body I will set upon your throne." Since we know that this Sunday is laying the foundation for Advent, which announces among other things the birth of Jesus, the Messiah, the notion of the Davidic covenant and lineage "makes sense." This is confirmed by the first reading in Advent 1 (Jer 33:14-16), which alludes to the "righteous Branch to spring up for David." So the first theme to emerge from the 2 Samuel has to do with the "typology" of David as the forbear of Jesus the King. It is placed in the first "box," after the synopsis.

But this passage also names the covenant with David as "everlasting." Since this covenant is a covenant for David's progeny, in the context of Advent and Christmas, this lesson is a forecasting and validation of Jesus' everlasting kingship. The third reading for this Sunday speaks of God's eternal nature ("who is and who was and who is to come") and connects it with Christ as the "ruler of the kings of the earth." This sort of theme is echoed again in the first and Gospel readings for Advent 4. The second theme is the everlasting nature of God's covenant with David/Jesus.

Finally the Samuel reading ominously speaks of the destruction of the "godless." Here the eschatological theme of Advent begins. It is echoed in the second reading (v. 19a, *The Book of Common Prayer*) and with the dramatic image of Jesus returning "on clouds" in the third reading. A quick perusal of the synopses of the other readings for the season finds that eschatological themes appear in thirteen of the sixteen Advent readings! Sometimes the end is seen as woeful, sometimes as good news, and sometimes as both, but it clearly is a major thread in the Advent tapestry. Hence our third theme for 2 Samuel 23:1-7 is "ultimate judgment" and in Samuel's case, "on the godless."

Box one for the Sunday of the Reign of Christ is now complete. It contains a shorthand synopsis of the text, three themes drawn from that text as it is read in the context of the other three readings for this Sunday, and the synopses of the texts for Advent and Christmas. The preacher's next task is to do the same thing for the remaining three lessons for this Sunday. The result would look something like this:

Step Two of Exegetical Chart for the Last Sunday before Advent
Reign of Christ Sunday: Year B

Lesson 1	Lesson 2	Lesson 3	Gospel
2 Sam 23:1-7:	Ps 132:1-13 (14-19):	Rev 1:4b-8:	John 18:33-37:
Last words of David. Davidic kingship-line. The Spirit of God speaks through King David. A just ruler pleases God; Everlasting covenant with David. Destruction of the "godless."	Song of Davidic history with God. Ark and God's presence. The Lord's oath to David: "A son, the fruit of your body I will set upon your throne." God's promise to establish Zion and David's line.	Grace and peace from him who is, was, and is to come and from Christ, first born from the dead and ruler of the kings of the earth. He made us a kingdom and priests serving his God and father.	Jesus before Pilate. Are you King of the Jews? My kingdom is not from this world. So you are a king? You say so . . . I was born, came into this world to testify to the truth.
Themes:	Themes:	Themes:	Theme:
1. Typology of Davidic kingship/Davidic lineage of Jesus. 2. Everlasting nature of God's covenant with David/Jesus. 3. Ultimate judgment on the "godless."	1. Typology of Davidic kingship. 2. God's presence with God's people. 3. Promise of a king of David's lineage and everlasting kingdom. 4. Intimations of judgment on the heir's enemies (v. 19a).	1. Almighty God has made Jesus ruler over all earthly powers; Christ has made us (church?) his kingdom (and us priests). 2. He is returning. Those who oppose him will be judged.	Jesus' paradoxical kingship, not kingship as derived or understood from the standpoint of (fearful, sinful, controlling, and so on) "worldly" human existence.

It should be noted that these themes are not the only or the "correct" ones to be found in these readings. Every exegete will find his or her own themes depending on the location from which she or he is reading. Nevertheless, most will find these basic themes, as well as possibly others.

Having thus "brainstormed" the texts and then having identified leading themes, we are in danger of thinking we are ready to go over the chart in order to identify homiletical options and to make the move to the sermon. Preaching ministers, often overworked and much too hurried, may want to get a sermon together for "this week." To incorporate fully the voice of the lectionary and the witness of the church year, however, these options should not be finalized until this Sunday's readings have been seen in the light of what is coming in Advent and in Christmas. The reason for this should become evident when we have completed this exercise through Christmas. In the meantime, it may be useful to look at some sermon options at this point, hold them in abeyance, and see how they look at the end of the process we are suggesting.

The themes of all four readings for Reign of Christ Sunday cluster about the heading "king" and its correlates: "reign," "everlasting," and "power." This certainly suggests a homiletical exploration of kingship in terms of the perennial question "Who or what rules in your life?" with all the nuances that question conveys.

The readings also suggest the theme of judgment, and the preacher is offered the idea of divine judgment. This, of course, can be addressed in any number of ways. The texts suggest a quite straightforward prophecy that those who oppose God (and/or God's people) will be doomed. This is commensurate with the first-century Jewish notion of a judgment day at a certain point in history in which the wicked would be punished and the good rewarded. This view was shared by the earliest Christians, including Paul and the writers of the Synoptic Gospels.

This Sunday's Gospel, however, suggests a paradox. First of all, Jesus' kingship is "not of this world." This does not mean that Jesus' kingship is to be thought of only in "heavenly" terms in the sense that this world is of no account. The temptation to interpret John in this kind of gnostic way has lured many preachers. Rather, it may mean that Jesus does not seek or derive his power from worldly sources and that, indeed, his power will be manifest precisely in and through an apparent victory for worldly, sinful power. The reign of God is not manifested through external force. In turn, this implies a different, typically Johannine take on judgment. As Pilate stands judging Jesus, Jesus is in fact judging him. The difference is that

Pilate is bringing judgment upon himself because, like the Pharisees in John 9, he was unable to see beyond his worldly expectations which include self-reliance and awareness of the "power rules" by which this world seems to operate. Thus Jesus says, "I came into this world for judgment so that those who do not see may see, and those who do see may become blind" (John 9: 39). This suggests that we are in a constant "process" of judgment, constantly being given the opportunity to "see" the truth or deny it. One way to understand this is to see oneself as choosing in all the small decisions of life to turn toward or away from openness, love, reconciliation, indeed, God. Certainly there are many other ways to address this Johannine view of judgment and power.

These are just a few of the many homiletic thought starters that the texts of the last Sunday of Pentecost generate in and of themselves. But as rich as they are, they do not yet connect with the seasons of Advent and Christmas of which they are prelude. The lectionary preacher will remember that her or his assembly will (hopefully) be in church not only this Sunday but the following four Sundays of Advent and then on Christmas Eve or Christmas and the Sunday following. During this time, the whole culture will be saturated with "holiday" celebrations and preparations. In Advent and Christmas the church will offer its gifts of preparation and celebration and suggest that as important and in fact blessed as Christmas gifts and parties may be, there is, was, and will be something deeper and more salvific working in the upcoming season. The preacher is called on to put her or himself in the stream of this narrative as a whole piece and to see each sermon as part of each liturgy, which is in turn part of one grand liturgy of Advent-Incarnation. Our hypothesis is that while the themes of sovereignty and judgment will remain, they will acquire new depth and breadth because they will tie in with these and related themes as they appear throughout Advent and Christmas. Thus the preacher will delay the fourth step of turning to the sermon until Advent and Christmas have been examined. The first three steps are designed to summarize the multitude of lectionary texts in such a way that they can be seen not only in light of their individuality but in terms of their seasonal unity.

In order to do this, we now turn to repeating the exercise we just tried out with the Reign of Christ Sunday for the whole of Advent and Christmas. The results of that exercise are distilled in the chart that follows.

Charting Advent—Christmas
Reign of Christ: Year B

Lesson 1	Lesson 2	Lesson 3	Gospel
2 Sam 23:1-7:	Ps 132:1-13 (14-19):	Rev 1:4b-8:	John 18:33-37:
Last words of David. Davidic kingship-line. The Spirit of God speaks through King David. A just ruler pleases God. Everlasting covenant with David. Destruction of the "godless."	Song of Davidic history with God. Ark and God's presence. The LORD's oath to David: "A son, the fruit of your body I will set upon your throne." God's promise to establish Zion and David' line.	Grace and peace from him who is, was, and is to come and from Christ, first born from the dead and ruler of the kings of the earth. He made us a kingdom and priests serving his God and father. He is coming with clouds, tribes of the earth will wail.	Jesus before Pilate. Are you King of the Jews? My kingdom is not from this world. So you are a king? You say so . . . I was born, came into this world to testify to the truth.
Themes:	Themes:	Themes:	Theme:
1. Typology of Davidic kingship/Davidic lineage of Jesus. 2. Everlasting nature of God's covenant with David/Jesus. 3. Ultimate judgment on the "godless."	1. Typology of Davidic kingship. 2. God's presence with God's people. 3. Promise of a king of David's lineage and everlasting kingdom. 4. Intimations of judgment on the heir's enemies (v. 19a).	1. Almighty God has made Jesus ruler over all earthly powers; Christ has made us (church?) his kingdom (and us priests). 2. He is returning. Those who oppose him will be judged.	Jesus' paradoxical kingship, not kingship as derived or understood from the standpoint of (fearful, sinful, controlling, and so on) "worldly" human existence.

Advent 1

Lesson 1	Lesson 2	Lesson 3	Gospel
Jer 33:14-16:	Ps 25:1-9:	1 Thess 3:9-13:	Luke 21:25-36:
"The days are coming" when the Lord will fulfill the promise of a "branch" of David. He will execute righteousness and judgment.	I put my trust in the Lord. Remember your compassion . . . remember not sins . . . remember me according to your love.	Abound in love for each other and all. Love each other, which seems related to God's strengthening "your hearts in holiness that you may be blameless before our God and Father at the coming of our Lord Jesus with all his saints."	"Little Apocalypse." Celestial and natural signs, foreboding, powers of heaven shaken. Son of Man comes in clouds with power . . . means redemption is drawing near. Parable of the fig tree. Sprouting leaves a sign of summer. The kingdom is near. This generation will see it. Heaven and earth will pass away, but my words will not. Be on watch. Don't be weighed down by dissipation, worries of this life. These things will come on the whole earth. Pray that you may escape and stand before the Son of Man.
Themes: 1. Prophecy of coming of Davidic ruler. 2. He will execute justice and righteousness	Theme: Trust the Lord to be compassionate and loving to sinners.	Themes: 1. (Implicit): Christ is coming in judgment soon. 2. This judgment requires holiness and blamelessness. 3. Loving is related to this holiness	Themes: 1. Judgment of the whole earth is imminent. 2. Judgment will be universal, cosmic. 3. Be ready, not preoccupied with or distracted by worldly things. 4. Christ's words are everlasting

Advent 2

Lesson 1	Lesson 2	Lesson 3	Gospel
Bar 5:1-9: Take off sorrow and affliction and God will restore Jerusalem and bring back refugees and God will lead Israel with joy in his glory. Or Mal 3:1-4: I am sending my messenger before me to prepare the way for me—the messenger of the covenant in whom you delight, but, who can stand when he appears? He is like refiner's fire and fuller's soap to purify.	Luke 1:68-79: Song of Zechariah. Blessed be the Lord, God of Israel who has come to God's people to set them free. God has raised a savior to save us from our enemies as God's promised . . . You my child shall be called the prophet of the Most High for you will go before the Lord to prepare his way to give the people knowledge of salvation through the forgiveness of sins . . . to shine on those in darkness and the shadow of death.	Phil 1:3-11: The one who began a good work in you will bring it to completion by the Day of Jesus Christ. Prays that your love will overflow more and more so that in the day of Christ you may be blameless.	Luke 3:1-6: Word of God appears to John, and he appears preaching repentance and baptism for the remission of sins: "prepare the way . . . [m]ake the rough way smooth . . . all flesh shall see the salvation of God."
Themes: **God will restore to state of joy.** Or **1. God's messenger is coming to prepare for God's longed-for "Day."** **2. But his coming will be a painful, purifying trial.**	Themes: **1. This canticle in Luke refers directly to the Baptist.** **2. John's vocation is to prepare the way for Messiah by way of forgiveness of sins.**	Themes: **1. Spiritual progress continues and will be complete by judgment.** **2. Love is (the/a?) means to being judged blameless.**	Themes: **1. John is the forerunner of Messiah (Christ) and the Day of the Lord.** **2. Repentance is the key to preparing for him.**

Advent 3

Lesson 1	Lesson 2	Lesson 3	Gospel
Zeph 3:14-20: The Lord has taken away the judgments against you . . . will gather the outcast and bring them home . . . will renew you with the Lord's love . . . will remove disaster and reproach . . . make you renowned among all people.	Isa 12:2-6: It is God who saves me . . . on that day you shall say give thanks to the Lord and call on God's name. Sing with joy and make God's name known and exalted.	Phil 4:4-7: Rejoice . . . be gentle . . . the Lord is near you. Don't worry about anything. The peace of God will guard your hearts and minds in Jesus Christ.	Luke 3:7-18: John's preaching repentance; the eschaton is near . . . bear good fruit . . . live ethically . . . Prediction: "I baptize you with water; but one who is . . . coming will baptize you with the Holy Spirit and fire." His winnowing fork is in his hand . . . the wheat to the granary, the chaff to fire. So John proclaimed the "good news" to the people.
Themes: 1. The Lord is about to act to renew the people with love. 2. The Lord has taken away judgments.	Theme: "That day" (the Day of the Lord) will be a time of rejoicing, thanking God, and making God's name known.	Themes: 1. The Lord is near. 2. Exhortation to not worry, to be gentle, and to rejoice.	Themes: 1. John is the forerunner of Messiah (Jesus). 2. The time of judgment is at hand. 3. The people are sinners who must repent. 4. The rule for this time before Messiah is to live ethically. 5. The Messiah will judge and gather in the saved and put away the damned.

Advent 4

Lesson 1	Lesson 2	Lesson 3	Gospel
Mic 5:2-5a: The ruler of Israel comes from Bethlehem. Therefore (God) shall "give them up until the time when she who is in labor has brought forth, then the rest of his kindred shall return to the people of Israel." He shall feed his flock, they shall live secure and he shall be great to the ends of the earth; "the one of peace."	Luke 1:46-55: "Magnificat": Mary's song of triumph. She proclaims the Lord's greatness for looking favorably on her. God's mercy is on those who fear God. . . . God scatters the proud in their conceit, casts down the mighty, raises up the lowly, comes to the help of Israel as he promised. Or Ps 80:1-7: Prayer that God would restore us, show us the light of your countenance . . . and we shall be saved.	Heb 10:5-10: When Christ came into the world he said to God, "sacrifices and offerings [according to the law] you have not desired. . . . I have come to do your will" (as was prophesied). We have been sanctified through the offering of the body of Jesus once for all.	Luke 1:39-45 (46-55): Mary goes to Elizabeth and John "leaps" in her womb. "Blessed are you among women and blessed is the fruit of your womb and blessed is she who believed that there would be a fulfillment of what was spoken to her by the Lord." vv. 46-55: Magnificat again, see Advent 4, lesson 2 above.
Themes: 1. Messiah shall come from Bethlehem. 2. The people will seem bereft until Messiah is born. 3. Messiah shall make his people secure, be great over all earth, and bring peace.	Themes: 1. Mary's thankfulness for regarding (choosing?) her. 2. God has remembered God's promise and has reversed unjust social structures. Or 1. Prayer that God would restore the people after a long time of suffering. 2. God is like a shepherd.	Themes: 1. God does not want the sacrifices of the old covenant. 2. Christ has come to do God's will. 3. Christ was prophesied, that is, was God's plan. 4. Christ's offering of himself (on the cross) once for all sanctifies us.	Themes: 1. John's in utero recognition proves Jesus' identity. 2. Honor given to Mary as the mother of the Lord (the place of Mary in the plan of salvation). 3. (vv. 46-55) God's reversal of unjust social structures.

Christmas Proper 1

Lesson 1	Lesson 2	Lesson 3	Gospel
Isa 9:2-7:	Ps 96:	Titus 2:11-14:	Luke 2:1-14 (15-20):
People in darkness have light, oppression has been broken, signs of war done away with. A child is born to us: Wonderful Counselor, Mighty God, Everlasting Father, Prince of Peace. He will establish the Davidic kingdom in peace, justice, and righteousness forever.	Sing to the Lord a new song, let all the world rejoice. The Lord is king and will judge (rule) righteously.	The grace of God has appeared bringing salvation to all. Live upright lives in the present age while waiting for the manifestation of Christ, who gave himself for us to redeem us.	Jesus born in Bethlehem in a manger because there was a census and Joseph was of David's line. An angel appears to shepherds and the heavenly host announces "on earth peace among those whom he favors." vv. 15-20: Shepherds go to see Jesus and relate what was told them. Mary is amazed and "ponders in her heart."
Themes: 1. Darkness and oppression done away with. 2. Messiah is born; a child.	Theme: The Lord is king.	Themes: 1. The grace of God has appeared. 2. The manifestation of Christ is coming. 3. Live right while waiting.	Themes: 1. Jesus is born a "poor outsider." 2. He is in the Davidic line, born in David's city. 3. It is certified first to "low-class" people by angelic manifestation. 4. Mary "ponders" the event.

Christmas Proper 2

Lesson 1	Lesson 2	Lesson 3	Gospel
Isa 62:6-12:	Ps 97:	Titus 3:4-7:	Luke 2:(1-7) 8-20:
Remind the Lord until God establishes Jerusalem. God has sworn freedom and prosperity for her. "See, your salvation comes . . ." They shall be called a Holy People, redeemed, and so on.	The Lord is King . . . Proclamation of God's might. A light has sprung up for the righteous.	When the goodness and loving-kindness of God our savior appeared, he saved us not because of our righteousness but his mercy, through baptism, so justified by grace we might become heirs to eternal life.	(The account of Jesus' birth in Bethlehem.) Angel and host appear to shepherds. They go to see Jesus and relate what was told them. Mary ponders this in her heart.
Themes: 1. Remind the Lord of his promises. 2. Salvation comes. 3. Redemption is/has come.	Themes: 1. God's sovereignty. 2. The "light" has come.	Themes: 1. Our savior came because of God's love. 2. We are heirs of eternal life.	Themes: See Christmas Proper 1.

Christmas Proper 3

Lesson 1	Lesson 2	Lesson 3	Gospel
Isa 52:7-10:	Ps 98:	Heb 1:1-4 (5-12):	John 1:1-14:
How beautiful on the mountains are the feet of the messenger who brings good news. The Lord has redeemed Jerusalem; all the earth shall see God's salvation.	Sing to the Lord a new song. God's might, mercy. "In righteousness shall he judge the world."	In the last days (God) has spoken to us by a son whom God appointed heir of all things, through whom God created the worlds. He is a reflection of God's glory and exact imprint of God's being and he sustains all things through his power-ful word. When he had purified sins he sat down at the right hand, higher than the angels. (Amplification and assurance of this for-ever).	The "prologue." The Incarnation of the eternal Word. John testified to him. He came to his own who received him not; to the world, which did not recognize him. But to all who received him and believed, he gave power to become children of God.
Theme: Redemption has come and all shall acknowledge it.	Theme: A new thing; God/Messiah shall rule justly.	Themes: 1. These are the last days. 2. God spoke to us through his son, the agent of all creation and the heir of cre-ation. 3. Christ's divine identity. 4. He has taken away sins and now reigns with God.	Themes: 1. The eternal Word through which all was created. 2. Became human "flesh." 3. The world did not recognize/ receive him. 4. Those who did received power to become children of God. 5. To see him was to see God's glory. 6. John testified to his identity.

Sunday after Christmas

Lesson 1	Lesson 2	Lesson 3	Gospel
Isa 61:10–62:3:	Ps 147:	Gal 3:23-25; 4:4-7:	John 1:1-18:
I will greatly rejoice in the Lord. My whole being shall exult in my God. God has covered me with the robe of righteousness. I will not rest until Jerusalem's vindication is manifest to the nations.	Alleluia! How good to sing praises to God who is almighty and redeems the lowly and broken-hearted.	The Law was our disciplinarian till Christ came. . . . In the fullness of time, born of a woman, under the law, to redeem those under the law that we might receive adoption as children. God is Abba so we are God's children and heirs.	See Christmas Proper 3 Gospel. Add: Law came through Moses: grace and truth through Jesus Christ. No one has seen God. God's only Son has made him known.
Theme: "Vindication" (the new era) is about to be manifest to all.	Theme: God redeems lowly and despairing.	Themes: 1. The Law was our "guardian" till Christ came. 2. He was born of a woman, under all human conditions. 3. The Incarnation enabled us to become children and heirs of God.	Themes: In addition to above, 1. Law came through Moses, grace and truth through Jesus. 2. God is unseeable. Christ has made him known.

Step Three: Mapping the Narrative of the Cycle

We are now able to look at the sweep of the narrative from the Reign of Christ Sunday through the First Sunday after Christmas. Our next effort is to see if there is an evident trajectory, not unlike the unfolding of the plot of a play, in the incarnational segment of the story of salvation. Again, we have in mind constructing a series of sermons that take seriously that the congregation will be living through an extended liturgy in which we will move from the Sunday of the Reign of Christ in which Ordinary Time is culminated, through four Sundays of expectancy and preparation to a time of rejoicing. They will experience the colors of the church changing from green to white, then to violet or blue, and then to white again. They will experience hymns that change in tone. They will, perhaps, experience four weeks of a solitary green wreath with four dark-colored candles followed by bright and often effusive floral displays, a decorated tree, and perhaps a creche.[1] They will move from rather somber services to what is for many the most moving and seriously joyful service of the church year, Christmas Eve.[2] One of the things the church is about is helping people understand that Christmas is not an isolated phenomenon in which the birth of the baby Jesus arrives without antecedents except for frantic cooking, shopping, and decorating. The nativity is a nodal point in a whole story, a divine, cosmic, and human process, which is going on now and in which we are all participants. The lectionary preacher always has an eye on helping people live into that narrative in order to understand their lives in terms of that process.

When we look at these lessons, we must remember that reading is always from our own social, theological, and personal location. Consequently the themes each of us discovers in these readings will be somewhat different. There are, nevertheless, certain overarching movements that most readers acknowledge. With these things in mind, what do we discover when we review the themes we have culled from these Sunday-by-Sunday readings? The following process of identifying and summarizing interconnecting themes for this season is the third step in our process.

Reign of Christ Sunday:	**God has promised a king in the line of David who will rule justly forever. Jesus is established as that king and holds the power of judgment.** That judgment is paradoxical and is exercised in some sense through the judgments and choices we make in our lives.
Advent 1:	**Judgment is coming; therefore be ready.** God's judgment will be loving but requires that we be loving and holy.
Advent 2:	**John the Baptist is the prophet of Jesus Christ, and we must repent.** Repentance may be painful and difficult. Love is the basis of spiritual progress and being judged well.
Advent 3:	**John's announcement: Judgment is *at hand* and will separate the saved from the damned; repent and live ethically. *But* don't worry; the Day of the Lord will be a time of rejoicing and renewing with love.**
Advent 4:	**Jesus, about to be born in Bethlehem, is the Messiah (Christ) who will bring peace, rule over all, and overturn social inequity.** The "Sunday of Mary" exemplifies the Christian response to God by faithfully responding to God's initiative.
Christmas: Proper 1	**Messiah (Christ) of the Davidic line is born; darkness and oppression are conquered; God's grace has appeared. But Christ is born a "poor outsider," manifested first to "low class" outsiders (shepherds).** The manifestation of Christ is coming.
Christmas: Proper 2	**Messiah (Christ) of the Davidic line is born. Salvation, redemption, the "light," God's sovereignty have come, and because of God's love, we are heirs of eternal life. But Christ is born a "poor outsider" manifest first to "low class" outsiders (shepherds).** Mary portends the future story of salvation by "ponder[ing] these words in her heart."
Christmas: Proper 3	**Redemption (Messiah, Christ) has come; Christ is the eternal, pre-existent, divine Word through whom everything was created and who is the heir of all creation. This Christ has become human ("flesh," Incarnation, human nature). The world did not recognize/receive him. Those who did became "children of God" (co-heirs with him).** Christ manifests God's glory. He has taken away sins and now reigns with God.

> | Sunday after Christmas: | **God, who redeems the lowly and despairing, is about to reveal the new era of vindication to all. The divine Word has become incarnate. The world did not receive Christ. Those who did have become co-heirs with him. The old covenant . . . our "guardian" has been replaced by grace and truth in Christ.** Christ makes the unseeable God known. |

Now some main themes of the period from the Reign of Christ Sunday through the First Sunday after Christmas have been identified (at least as read from this author's location) and condensed to the degree that they can be seen as a whole. It is time to think about how one would approach sermons for this part of the narrative. To do this it is important to first find the trajectory, the "plot movement" of the period.

It begins (Reign of Christ Sunday) with establishing that Jesus is the legitimate Davidic ruler of all things promised by God from the old covenant. This culminates both the narrative of the preceding year and the readings of Ordinary Time by returning to an eschatological reference. Interestingly, the theme of judgment foreshadows Advent and so the assertion of Christ's Davidic sovereignty is exactly where we will find ourselves at Christmas. Moreover, the paradoxical notion of judgment as self-judgment inherent in the Gospel for this Sunday (John's account of Jesus' appearance before Pilate) will find an echo in the Prologue to John as read at Christmas (his own and the world did not recognize him, but those who did recognize him have become children of God). Thus the lessons for this day not only conclude Ordinary Time but offer a synopsis of the next five or six weeks. This Sunday's lessons set the table for the great divine exchange in which God takes on human nature in order to raise it to the level of the divine by asserting the sovereignty of the One who will be Incarnate. Consequently any sermon on this Sunday, whether on kingship or judgment or some particular text in these lessons, should be nuanced in such a way that it adumbrates what the congregation will be living liturgically during Advent and Christmas. Thus while it may be very well to ask "Who is the ruler, the Lord of your life?" the question must ultimately lead to a "poor outsider" born a helpless baby amid animals in a cold barn, attended to by an unwed mother and socially unacceptable shepherds. "Who is Lord in my life?" must now attend to Mary's triumphant song that "He has brought down the mighty from their thrones, and lifted up the lowly, he has filled the hungry with good things, and sent the rich away empty."

Advent 1 is fairly clear: judgment is coming. How we are to be judged depends on how loving and "holy" we are. This raises questions about what "holiness" is. The fact that we are to be judged by how loving we are is at least commensurate with the idea that we "judge ourselves" through the decisions and actions of our quotidian lives. The notion of judgment being linked to love implies the possibility of somehow reconciling justice with love. This is difficult, as anyone who has raised children knows, and so it highlights the paradox of the Incarnation: the ruler and judge of all things is born an infant who relies for his survival on the love of human beings.

Advent 2 signals the appearance of John the Baptist, who is, among other things, a symbol of the "repentance" side of Advent. Repentance (and here one might look at "metanoia" as changing one's whole mind-set and way of understanding reality) may be painful and difficult. John is the prophet of Jesus Christ. Again, love is key to changing and consequently being judged well.

Advent 3 is preeminently the Sunday of John the Baptist. Judgment is *at hand* and brings the threat of salvation or damnation. It also brings the call (again) to repent and to live ethically. But there is also the exhortation not to worry because the Day of the Lord will be a time of rejoicing and renewing with love.

Advent 4 is the Sunday of transition from the eschatological message of repentance to the (perhaps also eschatological) announcement of the birth of Jesus (Messiah), who will rule over all and bring peace and equity. It is also the Sunday of Mary, who is the other symbol of Advent and who counterbalances the Baptist. She represents maternal love and the kind of faithful response to God's initiatives to which true repentance would lead. In this connection, it should be noted that the Song of Mary (Magnificat) celebrates, among other things, the radical realignment of social structures.

Christmas 1 celebrates the birth of Messiah (Jesus Christ). The paradox, of course, is that the Davidic Christ, who is God's grace incarnate and who *has* conquered darkness and oppression and made us heirs of eternal life, is born as a poor outsider, an infant at the mercy of his parents and others, manifest first to shepherds, who are "marginalized" members of Jewish society. The lessons include an allusion to the future manifestation of Christ, apparently in the Pasch. One is reminded that in medieval and Renaissance paintings of the nativity there was often a shadow of the cross cast across the creche, and of the third stanza of J. H. Hopkins' Epiphany hymn, "We Three Kings," often sung at Christmas, which portends Christ's bitter suffering and death.

Christmas 2 hinges on the same Lukan birth account as Christmas 1 and puts forth the themes mentioned above. The lessons allow slightly different nuances to emphasize that because of God's love we are heirs of eternal life. The lessons also contain the figure of Mary, who "ponders in her heart" the meaning of the angelic signs and message. As such she continues to represent human response to the events of salvation in Christ. As the one who holds and meditates upon the mystery of salvation, she stands as a type for all Christians who ponder the meaning of Christ in our lives and in the world.

Christmas 3 presents the Prologue to John instead of Luke's familiar nativity story. Hence, supported by the lesson from the Epistle to the Hebrews, the Incarnation of the eternal, preexistent, divine Word takes center stage. On one hand, there is the enormousness of the assertion: "God became a human being." On the other hand, there are the implications of the Incarnation as doctrine. Among these are the possibility that because God took on human nature, we can take on the divine nature. Importantly, the narrative stresses that the world did not recognize him, but those who did received the power to become the children of God. There is also the paradox that Christ manifested God's glory. The implication is that if one saw Jesus in the flesh, one would see only a human being, but this human being manifests the full mystery and majesty of the Divine, the *imago*, the Icon of God. Does that mean that whenever one sees a brother or sister human being one also sees a manifestation of God? If so, the idea adumbrated in the Sunday of the Reign of Christ that one judges oneself in every decision in every relationship is clearly asserted.

Finally, the Sunday after Christmas repeats the Prologue to John, adding the theme of the function of the "Law" (our "guardian," according to Paul) until Christ came bringing grace and truth and manifesting God. An implication might be that salvation is a matter of relating to God and other persons rather than strictly behaving in certain ways. This is to say that the Johannine Christ puts relating to others in love, which requires seeing others both realistically and sympathetically, as the hinge of salvation.

At the end of the first three steps, the preacher will feel confident in his or her knowledge of the particulars of individual lessons, the ways individual lessons combine to generate themes for the liturgical cycle, and the ways in which those themes in turn work to tell the narrative of the Incarnation.

Step Four: Lectionary-Informed Preaching

As a fourth step, we can begin to sketch out sermon ideas for Advent. The remainder of this chapter proposes one model for moving from lectionary texts to sermons. The reader must remember that these proposals derive from a repetitive reading of the lessons for nine liturgies. The goal of this model of moving from lectionary texts to sermon is to help contemporary people live into those foundational events of the Christian story in such a way that the gospel becomes the lens through which they see and make sense out of their lives and their world. For this the preacher must her or himself be immersed in the sweep of that narrative so that the sermon can draw congregants into the story and at the same time witness to the power and validity of that story to make sense of life and death. Thus the exercise recommended here is as much to form the preacher in the gospel story as it is to gain some modicum of control over a vast sweep of biblical material.

Whether one employs something like this "platform" approach or some other, the first three steps in the suggested process stand independently. The reader should also note that typically in this process, a good deal of the material in this "platform" stage will be deleted as extraneous. What is retained will be amplified. Thus what follows is meant to suggest one model of how the interplay of texts, theological presuppositions, and personal and social factors combine with the narrative trajectory of the Advent-Christmas season to generate sermons.[3]

"Working Platform" Drafts for Sermons

Reign of Christ Sunday

1. Today, the colors of our liturgical hangings have changed from green to white. This is the last week of "Ordinary Time" and it culminates with a statement, an assertion, a confession: Jesus is Lord over the whole creation.

2. Part of this confession is that we, you and I and everyone in the world, are under judgment. And if we look honestly at our world—indeed, if we look honestly at our society—and our own lives, that is not a warm, fuzzy idea.

3. Furthermore, our faith has always confessed that sometime we all will be judged, and Jesus will be our judge. We have been promised that Jesus will come to judge us, and we confess it every time we say the creed. Whether we imagine that this will be a great cosmic event when Jesus comes back on clouds or something that happens when we die, or by some other fashion does not change the fact that we are under judgment, and Jesus is our judge.

4. Next week the colors in church will change again, to purple. Advent will be here, and for most of December the church will be in waiting: waiting for Jesus, waiting for judgment.

5. And while we are waiting—perhaps wondering about the state of our world and the state of our souls, perhaps thinking of things like sin and repentance—even as we hurry to decorate and buy gifts and entertain and be entertained, it might be good to think of today's Gospel.

6. It is odd, isn't it, to have the story of Jesus standing before Pilate, standing with his hands tied, standing as an accused criminal for Pilate's judgment, standing helpless. What an odd story to read on the Sunday we proclaim that Jesus is the sovereign ruler of all creation and will come to be our judge.

7. Perhaps it was not Jesus being judged at all. Perhaps it was Pilate who was being judged, who was judging himself by the way he saw Jesus, by the way he treated Jesus. And in doing the practical thing, Pilate condemned himself.

8. I wonder if somehow that is how it is with our judgment. After all, Jesus does come at the end of Advent, not on clouds, but in a cold, smelly barn. He comes as a helpless baby. Perhaps that has something to do with our judgment.

9. I wish for all of us a blessed Advent, a blessed time of waiting, a blessed time of pondering our judgment. May it be among us in all our parties and family gatherings, not as a fearful thing hanging over us, but as a great mystery to ponder in our hearts.

Advent 1

1. A few moments ago at the entrance we started Advent by singing Charles Wesley's great hymn: *Lo He Comes with Clouds Descending*. That hymn captures the spirit of today's Gospel: Jesus is coming to judge, that judgment will take place in our lifetimes, and it will come suddenly, surprisingly, like a trap!

2. This does not sound like good news! And yet the Gospel also says that there will be a way to come through it OK. Paul's epistle reinforces this idea. Love and holiness are the keys to being judged OK.

3. This sounds like better news, but still difficult. Love—how to love, who to love, indeed, what *is* love—these are difficult enough. But when Paul starts talking about *holiness*, for me at least, things get pretty murky.

4. My first notions of holiness are notions of someone who is not really like me, someone who is above me, better than me, someone who doesn't get anxious about paying taxes and credit card bills, someone who is rather flawless, who probably would stoop to help me. And when they did, I would feel condescended to. And when I feel someone is condescending to me, my first reaction is to feel humiliated and resentful!

5. Every act of *giving* is potentially humiliating to the receiver because the *giver* has power over the receiver. I remember a friend saying that she would never ask her father for anything because she couldn't stand the look of triumph on his face when she did!

6. This is true even in the dynamics of forgiveness. *To forgive* means, literally "to give the future." To withhold forgiveness means to keep a sense of power, but it also means humiliating the one who comes, penitent, asking forgiveness.

7. Paul says holiness and love go together. And, surely, giving and *forgiving* are part of love and holiness. But here is part of the terrible bind of human sin. Giving and forgiving both involve an exercise of power. No act of giving or forgiving seems to be possible without someone

feeling they are in control or are being controlled. Giving and forgiving both seem impossible without someone having power over someone else, and then how is it possible to be really and truly reconciled, really and truly in love, really and truly whole, because wholeness is part of what holiness means.

8. And surely the Jesus who comes on clouds to judge us is holy and holds the power to forgive us or not. And we must submit to that holy power.

9. But what a strange season is this Advent. The holy one who comes with power comes as a powerless baby. The holy God to whom we owe everything, at whose mercy we are, joins us in our powerlessness and humiliation. His gift of forgiveness and love comes finally from the place of absolute powerlessness and humiliation: an executioner's cross.

10. So here is a great mystery. If forgiveness is to truly work, it must come from a place that is strange to us most of the time. It must come from a deep sense that the forgiver and the forgiven share in the sin. If the little brother could know that he cherishes his power as much as his stronger brother and if the older brother could recognize that his wanting to have power over his little brother is because he feels powerless in relation to his parents, then the exchange which is forgiveness could happen.

11. And this is what the all-powerful God is initiating for us right now as we wait and prepare for the coming of the judge, a powerless baby, who will suffer as a powerless human person.

Advent 2

1. Today marks the appearance of John the Baptist. Instead of a psalm we recited the "Song of Zechariah." Zechariah, you remember, was John's father, a priest in the Temple. He and his wife hadn't been able to have children. An angel appeared to him and predicted the birth of John and struck him unable to speak. After the child was born, at his circumcision party, Zechariah spoke, and his first words were the prophecy we recited. It says that John would go before the Lord to prepare his way, to give his people knowledge of salvation by the

forgiveness of sins. It prophesies the daybreak of a new day, a day of freedom from fear, a day of peace.

2. And then in the Gospel, John appears. Luke doesn't really describe him, but Mark and Matthew do. And he was a rough character. He appeared out of the desert, in the wilderness by the Jordan River, well away from town. He seems to have been pretty eccentric, wearing a camel skin tied up with a leather belt. He survived by eating locusts and wild honey. He must have been pretty intimidating, but nevertheless people flocked to the Jordan wherever he was. His message was baptism for repentance for the forgiveness of sins. He stands in the line of great prophets of Israel: Isaiah and Malachi and the others who tell of God's coming judgment.

3. So what is John's message?

4. First, the Lord is coming, so get ready.

5. Second, getting ready means having one's sins forgiven.

6. Third, being forgiven means *repenting* and having a ritual bath to signify this cleansing of one's soul.

7. Perhaps the key word here is *repentance*. I think that when we hear that word we oftentimes think it means "stop doing the bad stuff you are doing, and clean up your act!"

8. But that's not really what John the Baptist is doing. John is preaching repentance all right, but the word *repentance* is far deeper, far more profound than that. The Greek word for repentance is hard to translate. Literally the closest thing would be "change your mind," but that doesn't really get it. Repentance is more like "rethink everything."

9. Rethink everything you think about how you relate to other people, the people you work with, the people you love, the people you run into casually, the people who are different from you, the people who ask you for things, the people who frighten or threaten you.

10. Rethink everything about how you think the world operates. Rethink how you imagine the world as a kind of jungle where people have to look out for themselves first of all. Rethink the issues of greed and poverty.

11. Rethink the purpose of your life. Rethink how hard you work. Rethink whether you are doing what you really want to do with your life and for the people you love.

12. In other words, rethink, reconsider, and reevaluate every assumption you make. See the world, see others, and see yourself differently. That's what repent really means.

13. And then, if you are willing to do that, the question is on what basis, with what yardstick, with what glasses am I supposed to see things? By what am I supposed to measure things if I really consider giving up my old ways of looking at the world?

14. On one hand, those are lifelong questions. But perhaps there is the beginning of an answer in today's Epistle. Paul prays for his brothers and sisters in Philippi, those dear ones who may have been his first converts. He prays that their "love may overflow more and more with knowledge and full insight to help you to determine what is best, so that in the day of Christ you may be pure and blameless."

15. Love is not a one-step, easy, fix-all answer. But in the beginning and in the end, it is the answer. God is love, and God so loved the world that he gave his only begotten son.

16. God loved us first and loves us as we are and loves us eternally. But to be able to really know and appreciate how loved we are, we have to be able to receive that love, and you can't receive love without loving back.

17. John's message "Repent!" actually means to reconsider your life and ask, "Am I treating everyone I meet with love, or do I see them as a means to some end or other? Am I treating myself with love, or am I pushing myself to work too hard, drinking and eating too much, or not taking the time to love those who love me?" And the most difficult question, "Am I working to love those whom I do not know, but whom I really do

influence: the working poor for whom a raise might mean I paid a little more for my hamburger or the starving children in Africa for whom United States foreign aid might mean I paid a few more tax dollars?"

18. Real repentance, you see, is a lifelong opportunity to ask ourselves how well we are loving and to seek the forgiveness of God and others as we fail and the grace to love yet again.

Advent 3

1. You remember last Sunday John the Baptist appeared on the Advent stage. He came out of the desert, preaching for people to make ready for the Lord, telling them to repent and be baptized for the forgiveness of their sins. And in today's Gospel, John is back and seems to be in particularly good prophetic form.

2. When the people come out to him, he gives them a tongue-lashing! He calls them a "brood of vipers." He tells them not to count on being members of the right group to save them. He says, in effect, just because you are a descendant of Abraham or an American or middle-class or a Republican or a Democrat, don't count on that to save you.

3. He tells them to "bear fruits worthy of repentance." That is to say, if you claim that you have decided to live with love as the rule of your life, then it ought to show up in how you act. At the very least, it ought to mean acting honestly and treating other people with honor and respect.

4. But his message is also one of great urgency "Even now the ax is lying at the root of the tree." The Messiah is coming right away! And every tree that doesn't bear the fruit of love and honesty and respect is done for!

5. Here again is the harsh, hard, foreboding word of judgment. One of the great themes of this season. It is the reason our liturgical colors are dark. We are waiting for judgment. We know in our hearts that so much is wrong with our world. That we human beings have messed it up so much, our wars, our pollution, our dishonesty, our fearful desire for power, our injustice toward one another, and our failure to love—

in other words, our sin—deserve judgment. Who will be able to stand up and face the Day of the Lord?

6. But today's Gospel lesson, the piercing vignette of John the Baptist, is only one of four readings. All three of the others also speak of the Lord's coming, the Lord's near arrival, but their tone is different.

7. Zephaniah says, "sing aloud O daughter Zion . . . The LORD has taken away the judgments against you."

8. The psalmist sings, "Shout aloud and sing for joy, O royal Zion, for great in your midst is the Holy One of Israel!"

9. And Paul tells his beloved Philippians, "Rejoice in the Lord always: again, I will say, Rejoice. . . . The Lord is near. Do not worry about anything!"

10. What kind of contradiction is this? John is calling us a brood of vipers, and Paul is telling us to rejoice, the Lord is near, and not to worry about anything.

11. This thing that seems like a contradiction is at the heart of the gospel.

12. We all know that there is something terribly, terribly wrong in the world. There is too much suffering, too much anger, too much fear, and too much injustice. It isn't right. There is a part of all of us that knows this.

13. And so we spend a great deal of energy finding someone to blame. It's the young people who don't adhere to old-fashioned, work-ethic family values. Or it's my spouse. Or it's corporate America. Or it's the Congress or the government. Of course, it used to be the Communists, but the world is no better since they kind of disappeared, so now it must be the terrorists. It's terribly important to identify the enemy, the who or what is causing the world to be so wracked with pain and injustice, whoever is causing me to be in fear.

14. And the search for the enemy is fueled by a deep, dark suspicion that we are part of the enemy. Of course, I didn't cause the recent demise of

the stock market. I did not cook the books at Enron, nor did I blow up the World Trade Center. I am horrified, appalled, and angry about these evil things. My family and I have lost a good part of my retirement. But somewhere I am also haunted by a nagging question. Did not my greed, did not my fear of not having enough allow me to kid myself about a bull market that seemed to have no ceiling? Did not my fear and greed cause me to lose my sense of history and put my money in what many analysts were saying were overvalued stocks? And maybe, just maybe, my lack of concern about the standard of living and the quality of life for Middle Eastern youth has some little part in the rise of Islamic fanaticism.

15. And as soon as I admit that possibility to myself, as soon as I stop trying to make myself a completely innocent victim of the evil enemy (whoever he or she is at the moment), then I become open to judgment. And if I am open to judgment, I find that, in fact, I am a small accomplice in the world's evil. I am not a bad, evil person, quite the contrary, I am a well-intentioned but frightened, defensive, helpless-feeling person who finds himself to be part of the sinful human race. A brood of vipers is an intertwined family of snakes that is dangerous because it feels threatened by someone who has stumbled onto its lair. We are a brood of vipers because we are frightened, feeling threatened, feeling we have to protect and do whatever it takes to defend ourselves, even if that means hurting others.

16. And so I am judged. I have judged myself by how, in my fear for myself, I have treated others, much as Pilate brought judgment on himself by his practical and self-preserving treatment of Jesus.

17. But in the midst of this judgment, in the midst of the sinking sensation that goes with knowing myself to be an accomplice in sin…there comes another word: "Rejoice! The Lord is near. Don't worry about anything." Here is the gospel: You are under judgment, and unaccountably, incredibly, you are found acceptable, loved, even lovable.

18. But to hear that word, indeed, to know that Word who is the bearer of the word that I am loved and lovable, I first have to open that dark closet in my heart where I know, but try to hide from myself, the fact that I am an accomplice in the world's great sinning. It's the only way

to find that now, now and forever, I am an accomplice in God's great plot to redeem the creation so that in the end God and love will be all in all, in which we shall all rejoice in the Lord eternally!

Advent 4

1. Christmas is almost here! You can tell it by the combination of excitement and fatigue that permeates our culture. The stores and the advertisements have been building since—well, since Halloween! We've been, and many of us still are, shopping. We've been cooking and eating, and still, though it's almost here, it isn't quite yet!

2. We are still waiting, working, and looking forward to Christmas.

3. And so in today's readings are Elizabeth and Mary. They are waiting in that old and particular way that women who are "with child" wait. My obviously secondhand impression of this waiting is that it is like no other waiting. I remember a woman explaining it to me like this: she said, "In my deepest, most inward being something that is myself and yet is different from me is coming into being. I am making my baby, but in another sense I have nothing to do with it. It is just happening. And, of course, I can't speed it up or stop it." It was a kind of miracle, and she could only wait. She was excited and joyful and scared all at the same time. But she radiated a certain sense. I think the only word I have for it is exultation. She was quietly, pregnantly exulting. It was, as nearly as I could tell, a waiting like no other waiting.

4. As so is Elizabeth's waiting. She, a woman who was apparently past the years of childbearing, is now with child, a miraculous event, which has come with a prediction. This baby of hers, of which her husband cannot speak since he saw an angel in the Temple, will be the prophet who makes way for the Messiah. And now her cousin, Mary, a very young woman, pregnant in a strange, miraculous way, comes to visit Elizabeth.

5. And as soon as Mary walks in the house, the baby John leaps in his mother's womb. This is not just ordinary kicking, you understand: this is leaping! And Elizabeth's exultation breaks out as she is filled with the Spirit. "Blessed are you among women, and blessed is the fruit of your

womb." She understands the joy and exultation leaping inside her. The mother of her Lord has come to visit her!

6. And Mary is caught up in the spirit herself. I don't picture her as meek and mild here. I don't picture her as the demure young maiden who looks with great anxiety at the angel who came to greet her last March and announced that she was "Blessed . . . among women." And I don't even picture her as the brave young girl who looked that frightening, heavenly apparition in the eye and said, "Here I am, the servant of the Lord, let it be with me according to your word"!

7. No, now with Elizabeth I picture her, already heavy with child, draped in layers of clothing as women were in Palestine then, perhaps with some little bells attached to the hem of her long scarf, overcome with the exultation in the room, beginning to dance and sing,

> My soul magnifies the Lord
>   and my spirit rejoices in God my savior,
> for he has looked with favor on the lowliness of his servant.

And she's twirling now, spinning in her dance.

> for the Mighty One has done great things for me,
>   and holy is his name! . . .
>   he has scattered the proud in the thoughts of their hearts.
> He has brought down the powerful from their thrones,
>   and lifted up the lowly;
> he has filled the hungry with good things,
>   and sent the rich away empty.

8. The waiting of two pregnant women symbolizes the whole universe pregnant and waiting. As Paul would say: The whole of creation groans in labor pains waiting for redemption, waiting for injustice to be undone, waiting for the proud and powerful who serve only themselves and bring war and suffering and death to be undone, waiting for the ancient promises of God that there would be peace and love reigning in the world. The waiting that must just wait, but exults in the waiting for what is surely coming.

9. We await the birth of a new world, the birth of forgiveness, the birth of a new beginning.

10. A pregnant woman never knows exactly when she will give birth, and she never knows exactly how the birthing will go.

11. And so it is with us in our pregnant universe.

12. But like Mary, like Elizabeth, like any woman with child, we know we are waiting and we know that this new thing will happen.

13. And so even in the long, long waiting, even in the anxiety, we exult.

14. We exult and sing with Blessed Mary: Sing, sing, sing out my soul, the greatness of the Lord! Rejoice, rejoice my spirit, in God my savior!

The next task would be to use these "platforms" to write sermons for each Sunday in Advent. Typically this would be done Sunday by Sunday. Some of the material in the platforms would find its way directly into sermons. Most would be reworked and distilled. But the most important thing is not the method for final sermon construction but finding the intricate way in which the lessons for a season, in this case Advent and Christmas, weave an overall pattern, which itself is made up of smaller patterns. The object is to make preaching a part of that integral liturgical experience that lies at the foundation of the church year.

CHAPTER SIX

PREACHING THE EASTER (PASCHAL) CYCLE

The incarnational cycle is matched in the lectionary and liturgical year by a second major cycle, the paschal cycle, the cycle of the story of Jesus' death and resurrection. As was noted in the review of the history and development of the liturgical year (chapters 1 and 2), the celebration of this story is at the heart of the development of Christian worship. The Christian liturgy took its shape around the celebration of Easter (Pasch), the founding story for Christian identity. The celebration of Easter Sunday was replicated in the celebration of "little Easter" each Sunday and soon was followed by the celebration of the gift of the Holy Spirit at Pentecost. As we have seen, these single-day celebrations were expanded into liturgical seasons. The Easter season, the days between Easter and Pentecost Sundays, was the first season to be celebrated by the early church; the season of Lent, marking the days leading up to Easter, was the next season to develop. Both of these seasons, in combination with Easter and Pentecost Sundays, comprise the paschal cycle.

The continuity of these seasons and holy days is not always evident in contemporary conversations about lectionary use in preaching. Lectionary aids and resources tend to focus on the different parts of the paschal cycle as discrete units. Lent, Easter, the Sundays of Easter, and Pentecost are the divisions used to organize the listing of texts in the *Revised Common*

Lectionary. This mapping can mask that all these seasons comprise one liturgical cycle. A beginning point for preaching the paschal cycle is the recognition of the continuity of story, text, and traditions that runs from Ash Wednesday through Pentecost Sunday.

The importance of this cycle for the life and faith of the Christian community cannot be overemphasized. The mystery of Christians' redemption in the life, death, resurrection, and ascension of Jesus, which Christians celebrate each Sunday in worship, shapes the liturgical pattern of the paschal cycle. From the beginning of the Lenten journey through the culminating joy of the celebration of Pentecost, the entire Christian story is enacted in this cycle. This cycle brings the worshiping community into the reenactment of the great mystery of the Christian faith.

Through the reenactment of this great story, the lectionary and liturgical year also call us to attend to the ways in which Jesus' story informs our own stories. The paschal cycle tells the story of how Christians participate in and are shaped by the story of Jesus' death and resurrection. We can see this overlap of the two stories clearly in the season of Lent. *Lent* comes from the Anglo-Saxon for "lengthen," and the name aptly captures the season's liturgical and theological function. Lent "lengthens" the days in which the church prepares itself for the celebration of Jesus' death and resurrection. These lengthened days, forty of them, provide worshiping communities with an extended period of time in which to "try on" the story of Jesus' life and suffering and to discover ways in which that story reconfigures their own stories. The narrative liturgy of the *triduum*, the three-day celebration that unites the events from the Last Supper on Thursday through the resurrection on Sunday, dramatizes the events of Jesus' passion and death and so draws worshipers into the Jesus story as the story of their own lives as well.

The first celebration of Easter—whether that is at the Easter Vigil or the Easter morning service—tells a story of undiluted praise and joy. The Sundays and season that follow—the Great Fifty Days of Easter—enable the church to experience the newness initiated by the resurrection as more than a single moment in time. By continuing the celebration of the Easter joy up to the celebration of the gift of the Spirit on Pentecost, the liturgical year and the accompanying lessons in the lectionary signal that a new age has indeed begun. As in the incarnational cycle, eschatological concerns also are very present in the second half of the paschal cycle. The story of the Sundays of Easter and of Pentecost Sunday is the story of God's inbreaking into the world in decisive new ways. The power of death, the way the world's story is defined, is replaced by the power of life, and the celebration of Pentecost ensures that the story of the paschal mystery will carry forward in the church's present and future. The lessons from the Acts of the Apostles that serve as the first lesson in the Easter season (instead of an OT lesson) enact this dimension of the story: the preaching of the early church proclaims the Easter gospel for its life and mission.

The storytelling function of the lectionary and liturgical year means that each lesson has at least two sets of themes. The first derives from the point of view and claims of the biblical text in its own context, the second derives from the context of the lectionary itself. The lectionary preacher works in the midst of multiple options and obligations. We have seen this phenomenon at work in the Gospel lesson for Lent 4-C discussed in chapter 3 (the parable of the prodigal son), and this complex intersection of contexts and perspectives is found throughout the lectionary.

The third reading for Maundy Thursday, Paul's instruction regarding Jesus' words and actions at the Last Supper (1 Cor 11:23-26), provides a paschal cycle example of this complexity. This lesson is situated at the beginning of the *triduum* in the Maundy Thursday liturgy. The liturgy is a celebration of the Eucharist, and in some congregations it may also include the ritual washing of feet, reenacting the events of the night of Jesus' betrayal as narrated in John 13. In this liturgical context the Corinthians text receives its preeminent meaning as the text of the institution of the Lord's Supper. This context reflects the weight that the Corinthians passage has carried in the history of tradition, as a key biblical passage that connects Christ's presence in the Eucharistic elements with the words of institution that he spoke at the Last Supper. The Maundy Thursday context leads the worshiper to hear this text as explaining why we celebrate the Eucharist and as teaching that Jesus is present when we do.[1]

In its context in Paul's letter to the Corinthians, however, 1 Corinthians 11:23-26 is embedded in a long argument about the dynamics of the Corinthian church. Paul contends that the Corinthians are operating by the principles of the world, showing preference to those who have money and social status. Their actions undercut the redefinition of human community that is expressed in the idea of the church as the Body of Christ and as a sign of the approaching eschaton (God's new age). For Paul, the Lord's Supper was a manifestation of the unity of the church, which was in turn a manifestation in present time of the world to come. This understanding is not incompatible with the notion of Christ's presence in the Eucharistic elements, and it resonates with the themes of love and hospitality in the foot washing. But the Pauline context does bring a different nuance to hearing this text than the liturgical context does alone. Attending to the two contexts together can suggest an angle of vision for the Maundy Thursday preacher.

In addition to the preacher's need to attend to the multiple contexts that are overlaid in the intersection of biblical reading and liturgical context, a key element in the lectionary preacher's preparation is the ability to hold together a focused reading of particular Sundays and their individual texts with an overview of the trajectory of that part of the narrative to which she or he is attending (for example, incarnational or paschal). The larger context of the Maundy Thursday liturgy in the story of the death and resurrection of Jesus will shape a sermon on that day, as will the particulars of Paul's perspective on Eucharistic practice. Indeed, the particulars of Paul's perspective, originally offered in a context quite distinct from the Maundy Thursday context, become a fresh and valuable resource in this liturgical context. First Corinthians' attention to the way the community's celebration of the Eucharist is an extension of other community practices suggests an overlap between the church's story and Jesus' story that probably would not be recognized simply by reflection on liturgical context alone.

Charting Ash Wednesday

Chapter 5 outlined a method for holding together the narrative and theological sweep of the liturgical cycle with the particulars of individual biblical texts, and we approach the paschal cycle with the same procedure. As demonstrated there, the procedure is designed around the construction of a chart with which the exegete begins his or her seasonal preaching preparation. We will explore the paschal cycle by focusing on the texts from Lent, Year A, with some attention to the lessons that fill out this cycle. This cycle is too extensive to make it possible for each of its Sundays to be charted in this chapter. Some sense of this cycle's extent and sweep can be seen if one reviews standard liturgical aids. In *The New Handbook of the Christian Year*,[2] for example, the section of resources for the paschal cycle ("From Ashes to Fire: Lent and Easter/Pentecost") runs for 130 pages, compared to 53 pages for the incarnational cycle.

The texts for the Sundays in Lent are arranged as the Advent texts were, with the Sundays in Lent in a vertical column and the four readings for each Sunday set up horizontally. The first step in lectionary sermon preparation is to read through all the texts for each Sunday in the season at one or two sittings and jot down notes about each text as it is read. These notes are "first impressions"; the object is to get an overall view of the section of the lectionary in question. These notes provide a thumbnail sketch of each of the lessons.

The second step is the identification of theological and pastoral themes. The preacher reads over the thumbnail sketches of each passage in the chart and begins to note leading ideas or themes as they appear text by text, Sunday by Sunday. At the same time, the preacher should make note of any apparent incongruities that this or that text may present. Both continuities and discontinuities are creative for the sermon process. After some themes for each lesson have been identified, the preacher is positioned to move to the third step—to see what picture of the season emerges from the chart as a whole. How is the story of the season in evidence in what the preacher has noted in the lessons?

We will work through one set of paschal cycle lessons in detail, to show how the charting process provides exegetical, theological, and pastoral orientation to the liturgical season in which the texts are located and to the particular preaching occasion. We will use the lessons for Ash Wednesday, which are the same in all three lectionary cycles (Years A, B, and C).

Step One: First Impressions

The first step is to read through the lessons and arrive at one's first impressions. These may include key words and phrases, the structure of the passage, the form and type of the passage (is it a letter, a prayer, a story, or something else?). Key to this step is to become so familiar with what the lesson says that the synopsis one enters on the chart can remind the preacher of the whole passage. The chart, which includes all the Sundays of the season, provides a quick overview of all the lessons of the season, so that one can review them by reviewing the chart. From one perspective, this step is very rudimentary: the preacher is essentially reading for content, to achieve clarity on what the text says. Yet this step is essential because the more vividly the preacher is able to identify what a passage contains, the more easily he or she will be able to move to key theological themes. In addition, by reading through and charting the basics of the lessons of the whole season, the preacher gets a sense of the preaching context that the lectionary creates. The preacher is creating synopses of the lessons, a series of thumbnail sketches of what the lectionary season has in store for the preacher. The first reading for Ash Wednesday is Joel 2:1-2, 12-17:

Blow the trumpets in Zion;
   sound the alarm on my holy mountain!
Let all the inhabitants of the land tremble,
   for the day of the LORD is coming, it is near—
a day of darkness and gloom,
   a day of clouds and thick darkness!
Like blackness spread upon the mountains
   a great and powerful army comes;
their like has never been from of old,
   nor will be again after them in ages to come.
. . .

Yet even now, says the LORD,
   return to me with all your heart,
with fasting, with weeping, and with mourning;
   rend your hearts and not your clothing.
Return to the LORD, your God,
   for he is gracious and merciful,
slow to anger, and abounding in steadfast love,
   and relents from punishing.
Who knows whether he will not turn and relent,
   and leave a blessing behind him,
a grain offering and a drink offering
   for the LORD, your God?
Blow the trumpet in Zion;
   sanctify a fast;
call a solemn assembly;
   gather the people.
Sanctify the congregation;
   assemble the aged;
gather the children,
   even infants at the breast.
Let the bridegroom leave his room,
   and the bride her canopy.
Between the vestibule and the altar
   let the priests, the ministers of the LORD, weep.
Let them say, "Spare your people, O LORD,
   and do not make your heritage a mockery,
   a byword among the nations.

Why should it be said among the peoples,
  'Where is their God?'"

The Joel text is an eschatological text, pointing toward the seemingly inescapable inbreaking of God's judgment. This is evident in its language about the day of the Lord ("for the day of the LORD is coming, it is near—") and the sense of urgency that the passage communicates. The great army that v. 2 describes is an approaching horde of locusts that will devastate the land, and Joel interprets this natural disaster as evidence of God's judgment on the people. Yet repentance and hope remain possible ("Yet even now, says the LORD, return to me with all your heart"). The prophet urges the priests to assemble all the people (vv. 1, 15, 16) to ask for God's gracious forgiveness (v. 13). Repentance is all-encompassing—of the whole person ("rend your hearts, not your clothing") and of the whole community (the aged, nursing infants, even the bride and bridegroom in the midst of their nuptial preparations).

As we enter our first synopsis in the chart, the first reading for Ash Wednesday might appear as follows:

Ash Wednesday

Lesson 1	Lesson 2	Lesson 3	Gospel
Joel 2:1-2, 12-17: "The day of the LORD is coming." An eschatological text. Judgment is imminent in the form of a locust plague. The prophet believes that God's judgment can "even now" be turned into forgiveness if the priests gather the assembly to repent together in worship.	Ps 51:1-17	2 Cor 5:20b–6:10	Matt 6:1-6, 16-21

The second lesson for Ash Wednesday is Psalm 51:1-17. This penitential psalm has a well-known traditional superscription, "A Psalm of David, when the prophet Nathan came to him, after he had gone in to Bathsheba." The traditional setting of Psalm 51 at this famous moment of reckoning in David's life and career (2 Sam 12:1-15) draws attention to the elements of wrongdoing, self-awareness, and desire for forgiveness that characterize this psalm. One way to capture this psalm for the chart is to use the psalm's structure and movement to guide the synopsis. The petitioner, personified by the tradition as David, pleads for mercy (vv. 1-2), confesses his sin (vv. 3-5), prays for God's forgiveness and gift of new life (vv. 6-12), and promises to live in a new way (v. 13-14). The concluding verses of the lesson (vv. 16-17) summarize what has preceded: a renewed prayer and a recognition that the petitioner cannot move toward new life without God.

We can now add the first impressions of Psalm 51 to the chart:

Ash Wednesday

Lesson 1	Lesson 2	Lesson 3	Gospel
Joel 2:1-2, 12-17:	Ps 51:1-17:	2 Cor 5:20b–6:10	Matt 6:1-6, 16-21
"The day of the LORD is coming." An eschatological text. Judgment is imminent in the form of a locust plague. The prophet believes that God's judgment can "even now" be turned into forgiveness if the priests gather the assembly to repent together in worship.	"Create in me a clean heart." A penitential psalm traditionally ascribed to the person of David. Moves from confession of sin to prayer for God's forgiveness to the petitioner's promise to live shaped by that forgiveness.		

The third reading for Ash Wednesday is 2 Corinthians 5:20b-6:10. One first impression of this reading is that the beginning is not really the beginning! The lectionary begins the selected reading mid-verse (v. 20b), and that verse comes midway through a much longer passage (5:11–6:13). This makes arriving at a thumbnail sketch of this lesson difficult because the lesson is part of a much larger conversation. This is almost always the case with the lessons from the Pauline epistles in the lectionary. At this stage in preparation, the preacher should work to arrive at a coherent synopsis of the lesson as it is divided in the lectionary. When the preacher undertakes the actual preparation of a sermon for Ash Wednesday, he or she will need to integrate this synopsis into the broader Pauline context.[3]

In the first section of the lesson (5:20b–6:2), Paul urges the Corinthians to be reconciled to God (5:20b). The basis of his exhortation and the model for reconciliation is the life and death of Christ (5:21). This basis gives Paul's exhortation its urgency: "now is the acceptable time" for the Corinthians to accept the grace of God that is revealed in the life and death of Christ (6:1-2). In the second part of the lesson (6:3-10), Paul shows the ways in which he has enacted the ministry of reconciliation, modeled on the gift of Jesus' life. Paul's ministry is one of paradoxes, suffering, and rejoicing.

The Corinthians lesson is difficult to reduce to a synopsis, but its central movements between exhortation and imitation can be rendered in the chart:

Ash Wednesday

Lesson 1	Lesson 2	Lesson 3	Gospel
Joel 2:1-2, 12-17:	Ps 51:1-17:	2 Cor 5:20b–6:10:	Matt 6:1-6, 16-21
"The day of the LORD is coming." An eschatological text. Judgment is imminent in the form of a locust plague. The prophet believes that God's judgment can "even now" be turned into forgiveness if the priests gather the assembly to repent together in worship.	"Create in me a clean heart." A penitential psalm traditionally ascribed to the person of David. Moves from confession of sin to prayer for God's forgiveness to the petitioner's promise to live shaped by that forgiveness.	"Be reconciled to God." Paul encourages the Corinthian community to continue God's work of reconciliation. The time for this work is now. Reconciliation is defined by Christ's life and death. Paul's ministry of paradoxes models a ministry of reconciliation.	

The Gospel lesson for Ash Wednesday is Matthew 6:1-6, 16-21. This well-known lesson from the Sermon on the Mount focuses on religious practices that were common in first-century Judaism and remain common today: almsgiving (vv. 2-4), prayer (vv. 5-6), and fasting (vv. 16-17). Jesus' teachings on the three practices are all framed the same way ("whenever you . . ."), and each section contains a description of how humans perceive the act of piety and how God perceives the act. The key term, "reward," occurs frequently in this passage (vv. 1, 2, 4, 5, 6, 16, 18). The introduction ("beware of practicing your piety before others," v. 1) and conclusion of the unit ("do not store up for yourselves treasures on earth," v. 19) place one's relationship with God at the center of the religious practices. "Piety" is another word for righteousness, so the lesson both describes and prescribes the ways in which individual believers make visible their relationship with God.

Ash Wednesday

Lesson 1	Lesson 2	Lesson 3	Gospel
Joel 2:1-2, 12-17:	Ps 51:1-17:	2 Cor 5:20b–6:10:	Matt 6:1-6, 16-21:
"The day of the LORD is coming." An eschatological text. Judgment is imminent in the form of a locust plague. The prophet believes that God's judgment can "even now" be turned into forgiveness if the priests gather the assembly to repent together in worship.	"Create in me a clean heart." A penitential psalm traditionally ascribed to the person of David. Moves from confession of sin to prayer for God's forgiveness to the petitioner's promise to live shaped by that forgiveness.	"Be reconciled to God." Paul encourages the Corinthian community to continue God's work of reconciliation. The time for this work is now. Reconciliation is defined by Christ's life and death. Paul's ministry of paradoxes models a ministry of reconciliation.	"Beware of practicing your piety before others." A teaching text from the Sermon on the Mount. Jesus teaches about almsgiving, prayer, and fasting. The only reward and recognition for acts of piety comes from God, not what others think.

Once first impressions of the texts for Ash Wednesday are charted, the next step is to chart first impressions for all the Sundays in Lent. Although it may be tempting to move immediately into identifying themes for the

Ash Wednesday lessons, it is important that the preacher proceed with charting first impressions for all the Sundays of the season. This will ensure that the preacher has the whole season in view. After the first impressions and synopses of all the lessons of the entire season are charted, the next step is to identify themes as they appear, text by text, Sunday by Sunday.

In order to follow the application of all three steps to one set of lessons, the completed chart for Ash Wednesday and all the Sundays in Lent comes later in the chapter. Our discussion will proceed directly to identifying themes for the lessons of Ash Wednesday, building on the work found in the completed chart.

To identify themes, the preacher will attend to the synopsis of the individual lesson, the synopses for the entire day, as well as the synopses of the entire season. At this stage, the preacher already begins to place an individual text in the context of the other lessons assigned with it, as well as with all the lessons of the season. As noted in chapter 5, themes emerge from the lessons in relation to the specifics of that particular lesson, to the other texts of the Sunday, to the charted synopses of the rest of the cycle, to the setting in the church year, to the preacher's general biblical and theological knowledge, and to the preacher and congregation's experience.

Step Two: Identifying Themes

As we look for themes in the Joel 2 text, the appropriateness of this OT lesson for Ash Wednesday is apparent. The lesson is a call to the community to come together in worship and the occasion is one of repentance and fasting. The lesson also sounds a strong note of eschatological urgency in the face of imminent judgment, and this theme is echoed in other lessons for the day: imminent judgment and the need for repentance in Psalm 51, eschatological urgency as the basis of exhortation in 2 Corinthians. The theme of worship that is prominent in Joel also recurs in the Gospel lesson. The Joel verse, "rend your hearts and not your clothing," is an important link with Matthew 6. If we read ahead into the synopses of the OT lessons for the Sundays in Lent, we note that a recurring theme is the meaning of trust and faith in God and the community's relationship with God. The Joel lesson sets the stage for this theme by drawing attention to the centrality of communal worship and communal repentance.

In the context of the other lessons, of Ash Wednesday and of the entire season, as well as the particulars of Joel, clear themes do begin to emerge. Repentance is not a private act, but must be enacted in the communal worship life of the community. A thematic reading of Joel 2:1-2, 12-17 identifies the prophet's perception of the need for communal repentance in the face of imminent judgment. The place for communal repentance is in worship. When God receives the community's repentance, God will relent in God's judgment.

These first impressions are only shorthand for the complex dynamics of the Joel text. They do not touch on the role of the priests in worship, for example, or the significance of the symbol of the call of the trumpet, a call to worship and a call to battle. Nor do they begin to examine why the community needs to repent or the character of God who welcomes repentance. These will all be attended to in the more focused exegesis at a later stage of sermon preparation. These first impressions, however, do provide preachers with the equivalent of a compass point as they work their way through the other texts for Ash Wednesday and on to the rest of the texts for the season.

We have completed the first two steps for the first reading for Ash Wednesday—provided a thumbnail sketch of the passage and identified themes that will guide how we link this lesson to its companion lessons and the rest of the Lenten season. The preacher's next task is to follow this procedure for the remaining lessons of Ash Wednesday. The resulting chart might look like this:

Exegetical Chart for Ash Wednesday, Year A

Lesson 1	Lesson 2	Lesson 3	Gospel
Joel 2:1-2, 12-17:	Ps 51:1-17:	2 Cor 5:20b–6:10:	Matt 6:1-6, 16-21:
"The day of the LORD is coming." An eschatological text. Judgment is imminent in the form of a locust plague. The prophet believes that God's judgment can "even now" be turned into forgiveness if the priests gather the assembly to repent together in worship.	"Create in me a clean heart." A penitential psalm traditionally ascribed to the person of David. Moves from confession of sin to prayer for God's forgiveness to the petitioner's promise to live shaped by that forgiveness.	"Be reconciled to God." Paul encourages the Corinthian community to continue God's work of reconciliation. The time for this work is now. Reconciliation is defined by Christ's life and death. Paul's ministry of paradoxes models a ministry of reconciliation.	"Beware of practicing your piety before others." A teaching text from the Sermon on the Mount. Jesus teaches about almsgiving, prayer, and fasting. The only reward and recognition for acts of piety comes from God, not what others think.

Themes:	Themes:	Themes:	Themes:
1. Communal repentance in worship is necessary in the face of imminent judgment.	1. Repentance and confession of sin precede the prayer for forgiveness.	1. God's grace makes possible a ministry of reconciliation.	1. Inward disposition toward God counts, not outward appearance.
2. Inward disposition toward God counts, not outward appearance.	2. God hears our prayers.	2. Time is of the essence in the community's response to God's grace.	2. God's grace is our true reward.
3. God is gracious and will relent in God's judgment on the people.	3. God is gracious and grants forgiveness and the possibility of new life.		

A commonality of theological and pastoral concerns begins to emerge from these themes: the need for repentance in the face of judgment, the possibility of forgiveness, the centrality of God's grace, the community's need to put God's grace into practice for their own lives, and the importance of worship. Yet these themes are not uniformly presented in the four lessons: the notion of what constitutes judgment and reward is different in each lesson and each lesson has its own eschatological perspective. In Joel and 2 Corinthians, the inbreaking of God's judgment is imminent and urgent. That sense of imminence is not as pronounced in Matthew 6 or Psalm 51, but there is a definite concern with God's future judgment and reward.

One can already begin to see how homiletically fruitful the discipline of charting the season can be. Yet if we are to take the lectionary and liturgical context seriously, we must still hold in abeyance the move toward sermon construction until we have the whole picture of the season in front of us. Once we have provided thumbnail sketches and charted themes for the entire season, we can turn to the third step in the preparation process: mapping the narrative of the season as a whole. This will enable the preacher to see the wealth of lectionary texts in terms of their individual voices and their seasonal unity.

Charting Lent

First Sunday in Lent

Lesson 1	Lesson 2	Lesson 3	Gospel
Gen 2:15-17, 3:1-7:	Ps 32:	Rom 5:12-19:	Matt 4:1-11:
"But of the tree of the knowledge of good and evil you shall not eat." God places the man and woman in the garden of Eden with one command to follow. The serpent argues with the woman and persuades her that God's command does not need to be obeyed.	"Happy are those whose transgression is forgiven." The psalm celebrates God's forgiveness of sin. The psalmist's experience of distress, confession of sin, and joy at God's forgiveness becomes a model for others who seek God's forgiveness.	"But the free gift is not like the trespass." Paul's interpretation of Gen 3. Adam's sin brought death into the world for all. Christ's free gift and abundance of grace bring life for all.	"Jesus was led up by the Spirit into the wilderness to be tempted by the devil." Three temptations: food, personal power, and political kingdoms. Jesus rejects the temptation and relies on the words of Scripture for strength.
Themes: 1. Temptation tests how firmly we are anchored in the Word of God. 2. Obedience to God reflects the strength of our relationship with God. 3. God's word gives life, not death.	Themes: 1. God's forgiveness comes readily to those who speak honestly and openly with God. 2. Steadfast love surrounds those who trust in God.	Themes: 1. Human disobedience signals the power of sin and death in the world. 2. The power of disobedience and death is undone by the power of Christ's free gift of his life. 3. Our obedience now is possible because of Christ's obedience.	Themes: 1. Temptation tests how firmly we are anchored in the Word of God. 2. Obedience to God reflects the strength of our relationship with God. 3. God's word gives life, not death.

Second Sunday in Lent

Lesson 1	Lesson 2	Lesson 3	Gospel
Gen 12:1-4a: "I will make of you a great nation." God's call to Abram to leave his father's house and God's promise of blessing that will follow.	Ps 121: "The Lord will keep your going out and your coming in, from this time on and forevermore." A psalm of confidence in God's presence and God's care.	Rom 4:1-5, 13-17: "For this reason it depends on faith." Paul's interpretation of Gen 12. Abraham's faith is the model and Abraham's blessing is available to all by God's grace.	John 3:1-17: "No one can see the kingdom of God without being born from above." Jesus and Nicodemus, the Pharisee, meet at night and discuss the meaning of new life and new birth. Jesus speaks with many double meanings that Nicodemus does not always understand.
Themes: 1. Abram is called to leave behind everything he knows to respond to the promises of God. 2. God's call to us may precede God's promises. 3. We are called to trust God's promises of blessing and new life.	Themes: 1. God's care and presence can be trusted. 2. God's care and presence are cause for celebration.	Themes: 1. Faith is saying "yes" to the word of God. 2. Abraham is a model of the new life that comes from faith in God. 3. God's promises are secured by God's grace, not our actions.	Themes: 1. Jesus challenges Nicodemus to let go of what he knows and respond to the promises of God. 2. New life comes from the gift of God in Jesus ("from above"). 3. We need to look beyond our expectations to see the newness that Jesus brings.

Third Sunday in Lent

Lesson 1	Lesson 2	Lesson 3	Gospel
Exod 17:1-7:	Ps 95:	Rom 5:1-11:	John 4:5-42:
"Why do you test the LORD?" The people in the wilderness have no water to drink, quarrel with Moses, and put God's ability to provide to the test. Moses brings water out of the rock.	"Let us make a joyful noise to the rock of our salvation!" A joyful hymn of praise to God, the Lord of creation. The people are urged not to be like the people of Exodus 17, but instead to listen to God's word.	"Since we are justified by faith, we have peace with God through our Lord Jesus Christ." A key Pauline passage that describes God's act of reconciliation for humanity through Christ's death.	"Sir, give me this water." A conversation between Jesus and a Samaritan woman in which she moves from misunderstanding to understanding and faith, as she grows to see Jesus as a prophet and possibly the Messiah. She announces the good news of Jesus to her townsfolk.
Themes:	Themes:	Themes:	Themes:
1. Temptation tests how firmly we are anchored in the Word of God. 2. God's promises (sustenance in the wilderness) are secured by God's grace, not our actions.	1. We are called to trust God's promises of blessing and new life. 2. Obedience to God reflects the strength of our relationship with God. 3. God's care and presence are cause for celebration.	1. Through the free gift of his death, Christ has reconciled us to God. 2. Christ gave his life for us freely out of God's grace, not our merit. 3. God's grace is the source of reconciliation, love, and hope.	1. Jesus is the source of new life. 2. We are called to recognize Jesus as the source of new life. 3. We need to look beyond our expectations to see the newness that Jesus brings.

Fourth Sunday in Lent

Lesson 1	Lesson 2	Lesson 3	Gospel
1 Sam 16:1-13: "The LORD looks on the heart." Samuel is sent by God to find a new king. The first seven sons of Jesse are not chosen, but the youngest son, David the shepherd, is the Lord's anointed one.	Ps 23: "The LORD is my shepherd." A psalm of trust and confidence in God's caretaking. God is the shepherd, and we are God's flock. God's comfort, goodness, and mercy are celebrated.	Eph 5:8-14: "For once you were darkness, but now in the Lord you are light." A passage of moral exhortation to the members of the community. A call to live out its new identity as children of light and do what is pleasing to God.	John 9:1-41: "I am the light of the world." Jesus heals a man born blind and the healing leads to struggles over Jesus' identity. The religious leaders do not "see" what is before them, that Jesus makes God's works visible to the world.
Themes: 1. Do not judge by appearances, but look with the eyes of God. 2. A true shepherd-king is one who is anointed by the Spirit of God.	Themes: 1. God's care and presence can be trusted. 2. God's goodness overflows in all aspects of our lives.	Themes: 1. We are new people as children of the light. 2. We are called to live as children of the light, leaving old behaviors behind.	Themes: 1. Jesus is the source of new life. 2. We are called to recognize Jesus as the source of new life. 3. Do not judge by appearances, but look with the eyes of God.

Fifth Sunday in Lent

Lesson 1	Lesson 2	Lesson 3	Gospel
Ezek 37:1-14:	Ps 130:	Rom 8:6-11:	John 11:1-45:
" 'Mortal, can these bones live?' " A prophetic vision text. The valley of dry bones symbolizes Israel in exile. God promises hope and new life where there is only death.	"My soul waits for the LORD." A penitential psalm that embodies the move from despair to hope. God is celebrated as the source of forgiveness and the hope for new life.	"The Spirit of God dwells in you." The Spirit of God is the answer to the power of sin and death. It is the source of new life. The Spirit of God is available to believers because of God's act in raising Jesus from the dead.	"I am the resurrection and the life." The story of the death and raising of Lazarus embodies how Jesus is the source of new life. Death, which defines existence for Mary, Martha, and Lazarus, is overturned by Jesus' presence and promise.
Themes:	Themes:	Themes:	Themes:
1. God is the source of life where there appears to be only death. 2. At the point of greatest hopelessness, God offers hope.	1. God's forgiveness comes readily to those who speak honestly and openly with God. 2. Steadfast love surrounds those who trust in God.	1. The Spirit of God dwells among us and frees us from the power of death. 2. Through the Spirit, we will experience the fullness of the resurrection.	1. Jesus is the source of new life. 2. Death loses its power in the face of Jesus. 3. Through Jesus, we will experience the fullness of the resurrection.

Sixth Sunday in Lent (Passion Sunday or Palm Sunday)[4]
Liturgy of the Palms

Lesson 1	Lesson 2	Lesson 3	Gospel
	Ps 118:1-2, 19-29: "Blessed is the one who comes in the name of the LORD." A psalm of thanksgiving, traditionally associated with a procession to the Temple. Also part of the liturgy of the Passover meal. Celebrates God's steadfast love.		Matt 21:1-11: "Blessed is the one who comes in the name of the Lord!" Jesus' triumphal entry into Jerusalem. Two parts to the account, finding the donkey and the procession itself.
	Themes: **1. God's presence in the world is an occasion for praise and thanksgiving.** **2. The community is called to worship God.**		**Themes:** **1. God's presence in the world is an occasion for praise and thanksgiving.** **2. The king enters the city riding on a donkey, the animal of the poor and humble.**

111

Liturgy of the Passion

Lesson 1	Lesson 2	Lesson 3	Gospel
Isa 50:4-9a:	Ps 31:9-16:	Phil 2:5-11:	Matt 26:14–27:66:
"The Lord GOD helps me." One of the Servant Songs. The song opens with the speaker's faith, describes his adversity and persecution, and ends with his faith in God.	"Be gracious to me, O LORD, for I am in distress." Dynamic similar to the Servant Song. The petitioner's lament in the face of persecution and pleas for help do not diminish the petitioner's abiding faith that God will save.	"He humbled himself and became obedient to the point of death." A hymn that celebrates Christ's willingness to humble himself, become human, and die a human death. This death results in Christ's exaltation by God. Christ's humility is to be a model for the Philippians.	"Jesus cried again with a loud voice and breathed his last." Matthew's version of the arrest, trial, crucifixion, and burial of Jesus. Begins with Judas's agreement to betray Jesus and continues through the placement of a guard at Jesus' tomb.
Themes: 1. God's care and presence can be trusted, even in the midst of great suffering. 2. Obedience to God reflects the strength of our relationship with God.	Themes: 1. God's care and presence can be trusted, even in the midst of great suffering. 2. Obedience to God reflects the strength of our relationship with God.	Themes: 1. Christ gave completely of himself, to the point of death on a cross. 2. We exalt and praise Christ for this gift. 3. We are called to model our lives on the humility and self-giving of Christ's life and death.	Theme: This reading of the passion narrative brings Lent to a conclusion and marks what lies ahead in Holy Week.

With all six Sundays of Lent charted before us, we can begin to get a sense of the season as a whole and its place in the paschal cycle. Common narrative lines and common themes emerge from this charting. For example, the theme of trust in God that leads to new life rings from each of the lessons for the Second Sunday in Lent (Gen 12:1-4a; Ps 121; Rom 4:1-5, 13-17; John 3:1-17) and offers the worshiping congregation a hope-filled way to engage the season of Lent. Each one of these lessons alone speaks to trust in God, but when taken together, the four lessons provide a powerful witness to this theological theme.

These commonalities do not simply occur in the four lessons for a particular Sunday but occur across all the lessons for the season. Study the chart and note the regularity with which themes of obedience to God emerge, for example. This theme is obviously key for the First Sunday in Lent, in which the OT, Epistle, and Gospel lessons all deal with temptation, but this theme also occurs in the readings for the sixth and final Sunday in Lent, in the liturgy of the Passion. Obedience to God's Word is also prominent in the lessons about Abraham for the Second Sunday in Lent, and in the lessons for the Third Sunday in Lent that focus on Israel's testing God in the wilderness. God as the source of new life can be found as a theme for many of the readings across the Sundays in Lent; the theme of God's forgiveness and grace also occurs in many readings, beginning with the readings for Ash Wednesday. The theme of letting go of the old and trusting the new also occurs as a theme across many readings and many Sundays. These themes give biblical shape to the liturgical function of Lent as a season of preparation and Christian initiation. These themes draw the congregation's heart and mind to what it means to be a people of God.

We would not be able to recognize the thematic coherence that runs through the entire season of Lent if we simply approached each sermon one Sunday at a time. The discipline of charting the season for first impressions and themes makes it possible for the preacher to think about the Sundays in Lent as a cohesive unit with common narrative and theological threads. This charting enables the preacher to live into the season as part of sermon preparation, to see in advance the journey on which the Lenten lessons will take the preacher and the worshiping community. This charting also provides a means for the preacher's own spiritual disciplines during Lent, as close attention to the narrative and theological arc of Lent can enable the preacher himself or herself to enter more fully into this season.

The charting reveals the pivotal role played by the Sixth Sunday in Lent. The complexity of this Sunday and its place in Lent and in the paschal cycle is evident from the fact that the Sunday contains two distinct liturgies: the liturgy of the palms and the liturgy of the Passion. These two liturgies indicate the dual function of this Sunday: as Palm Sunday, it marks the end of the season of Lent; as Passion Sunday, it marks the turn toward the culminating events of Holy Week. The lengthy Gospel lesson for the liturgy of the Passion, the entirety of Matthew's Passion Narrative, does not simply foreshadow the events of Holy Week; it actually narrates them for the worshiping congregation. The events that are determinative for the first two days of the *triduum*, Maundy Thursday and Good Friday, are already incorporated into the Lenten lessons. Passion Sunday leaves the congregation at the same place that Good Friday will leave them, at Jesus' tomb.

The season of Lent ends at sunset on the Thursday of Holy Week. The liturgical time from sunset Thursday through sunset Sunday is known as the *triduum*. The importance of these days is well expressed in the *General Norms for the Liturgical Year and Calendar* from Vatican II:

> Christ redeemed us all and gave perfect glory to God principally through his paschal mystery: dying he destroyed our death and rising he restored our life. Therefore the Easter triduum of the passion and resurrection of Christ is the culmination of the entire liturgical year. Thus the solemnity of Easter has the same kind of preeminence in the liturgical year that Sunday has in the week. (Ch. 1, Part 2.1)

Although many Protestant churches will not include a celebration of the full *triduum* in their Holy Week worship services, all churches nonetheless have some sense of the days between Palm/Passion Sunday and Easter Sunday as a time set apart and of the sacredness of the story that those days invite the church to enter and relive. Preachers often agonize over what to preach during Holy Week, what to preach at Easter; but in reality, these days are the easiest days to preach. Since the events celebrated and lectionary texts read for the days so perfectly overlap, the preacher's main job is to get out of the way and allow the solemnity and celebration of these days to be experienced by the congregation.

The events of these days—Jesus' betrayal, his trial, his crucifixion, the empty tomb, the resurrection—determine the texts and the themes. Unlike Lent, when the texts are chosen thematically, in the *triduum*, the texts reflect the chronology of the season and the temporal arc of Jesus' last days and of the days of waiting and resurrection. There is a "you were there" quality to the readings and to the worship rhythm, and attentiveness to the lectionary texts facilitates the pastor's role in re-presenting these days for his or her congregation. The role of the preacher during this time is to make the paschal narrative vivid for the congregation through a wide array of liturgical and preaching practices.

Due to the length of the paschal cycle (running from Ash Wednesday through Pentecost) and the number of readings (lessons for fourteen Sundays, plus lessons for Ash Wednesday, Holy Week and the *triduum*, and Ascension Day), it is not possible to chart all the lessons in this chapter. We will include one final chart, the last Sunday of the cycle—Pentecost Sunday, as this Sunday is the climax of the whole cycle.

Exegetical Chart for Day of Pentecost, Year A

Lesson 1	Lesson 2	Lesson 3	Gospel
Acts 2:1-21: "All of them were filled with the Holy Spirit." Pentecost narrative of the gift of the Holy Spirit to the gathered community. Holy Spirit empowers people to speak about "God's deeds of power" in their own languages. Marks the inbreaking of God's new age.	Ps 104:24-34, 35b: "When you send forth your spirit, they are created." A hymn of praise to God the creator. Celebrates the diversity of God's creation (even sea monsters) and creation's dependence on God for life.	1 Cor 12:3b-13: "There are varieties of gifts, but the same Spirit." Paul celebrates the diversity of gifts that come from the one Spirit. All gifts work for the common good.	John 20:19-23: "He breathed on them and said to them, 'Receive the Holy Spirit.'" The Johannine Pentecost. A triple gift: the peace of the Lord, a resurrection appearance, the Holy Spirit that empowers the disciples for their mission.

Themes:	Themes:	Themes:	Themes:
1. The Spirit empowers the community for witness. 2. The witness is not mono-vocal; each witnesses in his or her own language. 3. The outpouring of the Spirit is the gift of God.	1. Praise is the appropriate response to the generosity of God's creation and gifts. 2. God's spirit gives life to all creation.	1. There is one God, one Lord, one Spirit—source of all gifts. 2. The Spirit empowers the community for witness. 3. The community's witness is not mono-vocal; each serves with his or her own distinct gifts from God.	1. The gift of the Spirit fulfills the promise of the resurrection. 2. The Spirit empowers the community for witness. 3. The community is empowered to continue Jesus' mission.

As the first impressions and themes in the above chart suggest, Pentecost Sunday is pivotal both for its place as the culmination of the Easter season and for the way it opens up the worshiping community to the season of Ordinary Time. Not surprisingly, each of the four lessons has themes that revolve around the gift of the Holy Spirit, but careful reading of the lessons shows how the Pentecost gift is the climax of God's promises that the paschal cycle celebrates. This connection is clearest in the lesson from the Gospel of John, in which the risen Jesus breathes the Holy Spirit on his disciples, but the connection is also clear in the eschatological perspective that the Acts lesson, through its use of the Joel 2 text, gives to the gift of the Spirit. The gift of the Spirit empowers the community to live fully into and out of God's promises of a new age; the community that the Spirit forms and empowers is the community of the Resurrected One. Both the Acts and the 1 Corinthians lessons show that this newly created community is rich and diverse, just like the diversity of God's creation that is celebrated in Psalm 104. Pentecost Sunday puts all of God's gifts and promises before the congregation and as such is a fitting end to the Easter-Pentecost season. This Sunday also marks the way forward, because the community that lives its faith in Ordinary Time is the community empowered by the gift of the Holy Spirit.

Step Three: Mapping the Narrative of the Cycle

Our next step, as with the incarnational cycle, is to see if there is an evident trajectory, the unfolding of a narrative line, in the paschal cycle of the story of salvation. As a congregation moves from Ash Wednesday through the celebration of Easter and on to Pentecost, through what narrative are they living? What do we learn when we review the themes that we have culled from the Sunday-by Sunday readings that we have charted? Identifying and summarizing these themes reveals the shape that the preacher has seen for the season.

1. Ash Wednesday:	**Inward disposition toward God counts, not outward appearance. God's grace makes possible a ministry of reconciliation.** The community is called to prepare itself for a season of repentance, grounded in the assured grace of God's forgiveness.
2. Lent 1:	**Obedience to God reflects the strength of our relationship to God.** As we begin our Lenten journey, we know that God's Word gives life, but through our actions and decisions, we nonetheless may put our relationship with God to the test.
3. Lent 2:	**We are called to trust God's promises.** God's promises may summon us to places that we have not anticipated, and our faith in God empowers us for this journey.
4. Lent 3:	**God's promises are secured by God's grace, not our actions. Jesus is the source of new life.** The themes of obedience and grace continue. The Lenten journey is a balance of God's gift and our response.
5. Lent 4:	**Do not judge by appearances, but judge with the eyes of God. We are called to recognize Jesus as the source of new life.** The theme of discernment is now added to those of obedience and grace, suggesting that part of the Lenten journey is to acquire a new way of seeing God's place in our world.
6. Lent 5:	**God is the source of life where there appears to be only death.** The Lenten journey draws the community closer to the struggle between life and death, hope and hopelessness and points to God as the power of life over death.

7. Lent 6: Liturgy of the Palms:	**God's presence in the world is an occasion for thanksgiving and praise.** This Sunday begins with celebration of the "one who comes in the name of the Lord." Lent includes the celebration of God-with-us.
Liturgy of the Passion:	**Obedience to God reflects the strength of our relationship with God. In obedience, Christ gave completely of himself, to the point of death on a cross.** Christ's obedience opens for us the possibility of new relationships with God and with one another, based in obedience and faith. The community's Lenten journey brings it to the cross. These common themes are followed by the story of Jesus' death, resurrection, and ascension, leading to the climax of Pentecost.
Day of Pentecost:	**The gift of God's life-giving Spirit empowers the community for witness.** The gift of the Spirit fulfills the promise of the resurrection and empowers the church to live as an Easter people.

This condensing of themes enables the preacher to see the season whole. While a preacher may be tempted to skip this step in the interest of time, it is an essential part not only of the preparation for lectionary preaching but also of a preacher's own Lenten spiritual discipline. It is easy for the preacher to lose sight of his or her own spiritual and theological nurture, especially in a season as busy for the pastor as Lent, Holy Week, and Easter. This third step of narrating the season can provide the pastor with a way of locating his or her entire ministry during this season within the Lenten story. With these themes in front of us, we can begin to tell the paschal story of Year A.

Ash Wednesday establishes the contours of the Lenten season and names the journey that the entire congregation will undertake together in worship. Everyone is called to prepare himself or herself for the Lenten cycle. The texts' focus on repentance and communal worship underscores that all of us need to take this journey anew each Lent. Regardless of where one was in the previous Lent, each year provides the occasion for a fresh opening of oneself and one's community to God. The Lenten story begins by reminding the community of the need to turn in faith away from what separates one from God and to turn toward the fullness of God known through God's forgiveness. Interestingly, the narrative trajectory on Ash Wednesday does not start with the story of Jesus, but with the story of the worshiping community that needs to turn to God anew.

The Gospel lesson for the First Sunday in Lent is the temptation narrative in each year of the RCL, but the other lessons with which it is joined shape this lesson for each particular Lenten cycle. The discipline of charting and identifying themes becomes acutely important with familiar texts like the temptation, because going through these steps (or something like them) makes it difficult to simply assume that one "knows" what the familiar text has to offer. The combination of the temptation narrative with Genesis 2 and Romans 5 highlights the theme of obedience and this theme, as we have seen, will continue throughout Lent, Year A. The homiletical catch here is to see this Sunday with its focus on temptation and obedience as a story of hopefulness, not a story of human failing and weakness. The lessons provide the lens for the congregation to think about temptation anew, strengthened by the model of Jesus' obedience.

This theme of obedience and trust is the main narrative line of the Sundays in Lent in Year A. Lent 2 combines this theme with the other dominant theme of Lent A—that of journey. Abraham's response to God's call to go to an unknown place provides the model for the worshiping community in Lent: to go where God calls, even if God calls to the unexpected. This is also the challenge of the John 3 lesson: can Nicodemus imagine the new life that Jesus makes available and "journey" from the familiar to the unknown? The community moves deeper into encountering the new dimensions of trust that Lent will require.

Lent 3 moves the narrative line forward by telling another story of temptation (Exod 17), which makes vivid the temptation to distrust God and to doubt God's promises. This Sunday is an important moment in the Lenten story because it is a reminder that the Lenten journey is not without difficulties. It is one thing to talk about trusting God's promises; it is another thing to live on the basis of them. The story of the Samaritan woman is also a story of trust in promises that surprise because the Messiah that she expected is not the Messiah that she encountered and her act of faith is to recognize the difference.

As noted above, Lent 4 adds the theme of discernment to the themes of trust and obedience. This theme increases the sense of responsibility for the individual and the community on the Lenten journey because the texts ask the community to look beyond what is obvious in order to see the presence and call of God. The stories of the call of David and of the blind man in John 9 both emphasize the need to look beyond appearances and to judge by what can be discerned through a heart turned toward God. The Ephesians lesson adds to the story the sense that discernment will lead to fuller obedience and the ability to live out one's faith in action. The Lenten cycle deepens the narrative of journey and preparation as the season proceeds.

The Lenten story makes an important turn on Lent 5, moving the focus away from the community's preparation and toward the God who is the end point of the journey. These lessons sound a strong and unified theme and story line of God as the source of life where there only appears to be death, and of the powerlessness of death in the face of God's power for life. For the Lenten story, the climactic example of God's power over death is the resurrection of Jesus, and the John 11 story brings that example explicitly into the Lenten story. John 11 prepares the reader for the events that lie ahead—death and resurrection—by reminding the community that Jesus' presence and promise overturn the power of death. It is important, however, that the preacher not rush to preach resurrection on this Sunday, as that would disrupt the unfolding of the Lenten story. Rather, this Sunday's signal contribution to the Lenten story is the way that it forces the community to look death in the face. Something is at stake in the Lenten journey; we are called to trust and obedience for a reason, and that reason is to enable us to confront the power of death, which, if unchecked, can close us to the presence and promise of God.

Lent 6 carries two different parts of the Lenten story. One is the narrative of celebration at the presence of God. This is a key piece of the Lenten narrative, as the community has been preparing itself to be more fully God's people. Just as Lent 5 enables the community to see the power of God in the world, in the face of all obstacles, Lent 6 begins by giving the community the opportunity to praise and celebrate the One who has lived among them as the presence of God, marking the inbreaking of God's time. Lent 6 will make the decisive turn toward the narrative of the Passion, but before it does that it stops to celebrate the life and mission of Jesus, God-with-us. This celebration takes on an added poignancy, as the same Sunday will also narrate the full story of Jesus' death, but the Sunday insists that the community look at Jesus' life and death together.

The above narrative is one preacher's reading of the Lenten narrative cycle; each preacher will find his or her own themes and will tell the story in a slightly different way, depending on the circumstances of the worshiping community and the world at any given Lent. What is key for effective and faithful lectionary preaching is that each preacher take the time to tell the overarching Lenten narrative before moving to the creation of individual sermons. Due to the number of texts in the paschal cycle, this chapter has abbreviated charting all of them, using the Sundays in Lent as the model for what to do with the entire cycle. That means that for this chapter, the narrative of the rest of the paschal cycle is represented by the themes and story of the Day of Pentecost, the climax of the paschal cycle.

On the one hand, the themes and narrative line of the Day of Pentecost are self-evident: Pentecost marks the gift of the Spirit. On the other hand, though, as a result of charting the season, the preacher sees that Pentecost does not exist in isolation, but stands as the culmination of the paschal cycle. The gift of the Spirit does mark a beginning, but it is a beginning completely shaped by and grounded in all that has preceded it. The themes highlight the ways in which Pentecost is the theological and narrative climax of the paschal cycle—the Easter joy is made a permanent part of the life of the worshiping community through the gift of the Spirit. The fulfillment of God's promises is not limited to one moment in time, but these promises are ever renewed in the present and future through the Spirit.

Interwoven into this narrative trajectory of the paschal cycle is the narrative line created by time itself. As we noted at the beginning of the chapter, the paschal cycle has a temporal heft to it that is unlike any other liturgical season: forty days in Lent, the *triduum*, the Great Fifty Days of Easter. All in all, the paschal cycle runs over three months. This temporal heft means that to live this cycle is to have a significant part of one's year shaped by these stories and these theological themes. Time is calculated by reference to the paschal mystery, so that living through the entirety of this season ensures that the worshiping community has its life reformed by the death and resurrection of Christ.

This great extent of time also has a pointed temporal arc, with the *triduum* as the hinge around which the season moves. The *triduum* is that to which Lent points and from which the Easter season derives. The *triduum* embodies the core paschal gospel of death and resurrection. The forty days in Lent are the preparation for the *triduum*, and the Great Fifty Days of Easter are the living out of the paschal mystery of the *triduum*. The direction of the temporal arc is set by the narrative of the paschal mystery—from Passion to death to resurrection to ascension to the gift of the Holy Spirit. None of the narrative and temporal elements can be taken out of sequence—prior to the *triduum*, the community's life moves forward to that event; after the *triduum*, the community's life moves forward from that event.

At the end of these three steps—reading for first impressions, identifying themes, mapping the narrative of the cycle—the preacher will feel confident in his or her knowledge of the particulars of individual lessons, the way lessons combine to generate themes for the cycle, and the ways in which those themes in turn work to tell the narrative of the paschal cycle.

Step Four: Lectionary-Informed Preaching

When the preacher turns from this chart to actual sermon crafting, his or her own methods for creating and writing sermons come fully into play. Chapter 5 suggested a fourth step, that of constructing "sermon platforms" as the next stage in moving from the three steps of the chart to an actual sermon, but that approach will not fit all preachers. Whatever approach the preacher takes, it is important to remember that the seasonal chart is the beginning of the homiletical conversation between the lessons and the liturgical context. The preacher will need to return to each of the lessons in a more focused way, to determine which textual voice will give its accents to the sermon, as well as to attend to the ways in which the pastoral needs and situation of church and world inform the shape the seasonal themes will take in the sermon.

The first three steps are preparatory work for preaching through the season and do not constitute the full textual and pastoral engagement necessary for the construction of each individual sermon. Charting the season provides a disciplined way to hold together the narrative and theological sweep of the season and the particulars of individual lessons and to keep both always before the preacher. They are the beginning, not the end, of the sermon preparation process. With these three steps completed—and completed well before the individual Sundays of the season begin—the preacher can then move to craft each week's sermon in turn.

For preachers who are used to thinking of sermons and sermon preparation Sunday by Sunday, and not with a seasonal perspective, the charting recommended here may seem like more work than the busy preacher has time for. But, in fact, this charting (or some exercise like it) actually enables the lectionary preacher to use his or her sermon preparation time much more effectively and efficiently. A few concentrated blocks of study, prior to the beginning of the incarnational and paschal cycles, is all that is necessary for the preacher to complete the first three steps recommended here. This study can be done at any time during the year—during time spent away for continuing education, during the quieter summer months, and so on. With seasonal charts in hand, as well as the map of the cycle's narrative arc, the preacher who completes this exercise in advance has a significant head start on the preparation of individual sermons and, indeed, has taken some pressure off the weekly sermon preparation during these cycles. The preacher who is able to see the details and sweep of the cycle whole, who is confident about the season, is better able to focus individual sermon preparation time on the intersection of the lessons with the needs and hopes of a congregation for whom the good news is proclaimed.

And, most important, this method also enhances the preacher's own theological and spiritual formation. He or she comes increasingly to understand and experience the ways in which his or her story belongs to the common Christian story. As the Christian story becomes the lens through which the preacher views his or her own life, it increasingly and more profoundly becomes the lens and language that inform the telling of the congregation's story. The lectionary preacher's sermons can draw the congregation into the sweep of the Christian story—first the incarnational cycle, followed in the church year by the paschal cycle—and witness to the power of that story to make sense of life and death.

CHAPTER SEVEN

PREACHING IN ORDINARY TIME

The incarnational and paschal cycles narrate the core stories of the Christian faith—Advent to Christmas, Lent to Pentecost. As we have seen in the review of the lectionary's history and in the sample chartings of these two cycles, the readings for these cycles reflect the narrative and theological emphases of the expectation of the inbreaking of the kingdom of God in the person of Jesus Christ (the incarnational cycle) and the paschal mystery of the death, resurrection, and ascension of Christ (the paschal cycle). By living these two cycles through the preaching and liturgy of the church, each year Christian communities experience the whole narrative of salvation.

These two cycles are concentrated in the first half of the Christian year, and the swath of time from Advent to Pentecost is approximately six months. What happens liturgically in the remainder of the Christian year? In the Roman Catholic calendar, on which the *Revised Common Lectionary* is based, the weeks of the Christian year not included in these two main cycles are referred to as "Sundays of the Year" or "Sundays in Ordinary Time." There are two blocks of Ordinary Time: the weeks between Epiphany and Ash Wednesday (the transition from Christmas to Lent) and the weeks that run from Pentecost to the end of the liturgical year.

"Ordinary" comes from the word *ordinal* and means "counted" or "numbered." The numbering of Sundays in Ordinary Time is evident in the RCL listing of lections. The Sundays between Epiphany and Ash

Wednesday are numbered as the "Sundays after Epiphany": first, second, third, and so on. The Sundays after Pentecost continue that numerical sequence.[1] Note that in this counting, the emphasis falls on "Sunday." That emphasis is a reminder that at the heart of Christian worship is the central observance of the Lord's Day. The Sundays that fall outside of the incarnational and paschal cycles are not understood as a liturgical season, in the same way that Easter and Christmas are seasons, but receive their liturgical importance from their regular, indeed, numbered, celebration of the Lord's Day. Sunday after Sunday, the focus is not on the reenactment of the particular stories of the incarnational and paschal mysteries, but on the many facets of the Christian story as known through scripture and the worship and mission life of the church. The Sundays of Ordinary Time do for each week what the liturgical seasons of Advent/Christmas and Lent/Easter/Pentecost do for the year—they make the counting of time sacred. Even the succession of "ordinary" weeks in Ordinary Time is counted in relationship to worship.

The New Handbook of the Christian Year helpfully articulates the liturgical and theological significance of the Sundays of Ordinary Time: "The preeminence of the Lord's Day indicates the presence of the risen Christ in all our experience. The resurrection punctuates our perception of time by its commemoration once every seven days, regardless of what else may be occurring in the church calendar or in our own lives."[2] As crucial as the story narrated and enacted in the two central cycles is to Christian life and faith, the weekly celebration of the Lord's Day remains the defining liturgical moment. This means that Ordinary Time is not liturgical "down time" for the church but is a time when the church regularly reaffirms that God defines all time and all moments of Christian life.

Text Selection in Ordinary Time

In the incarnational and paschal cycles, the readings are chosen according to the principle of selected reading (*lectio selecta*). The selection of lessons is governed by the time in the liturgical season: the Gospel lesson establishes the theme for the Sunday, and the other lessons are selected in relationship to the Gospel text. The charts for the incarnational and paschal cycles highlight this principle of selected reading. Because the lessons are selected to go together, it is possible to identify themes for each Sunday, as well as for the entire season.

In Ordinary Time, a different principle of text selection is at work. In Ordinary Time, the lessons are chosen according to a pattern of semi-continuous reading. This principle of text selection, like *lectio selecta*, has its origins in an ancient liturgical practice, the continuous reading (*lectio continua*) of the synagogue and early church. In ancient synagogue worship, the Torah was read continuously in worship as part of the lectionary cycle: on each consecutive Sabbath, a portion of the Torah was read, each week's passage following in sequence from the passage that was read the week before. This pattern of continuous reading was carried from the synagogue into the early church.

One can find evidence of this pattern of continuous reading in the sermons of the early church. Most of the sermon collections that are extant from the third and fourth centuries are in the form of sequential readings of biblical books, and indeed, most of the early commentaries began as series of homilies on biblical books. The sermons of Origen and Chrysostom on the Gospel of John provide good examples of sequential, continuous reading. These sermons take their content and their form by following the biblical book, verse by verse, Sunday by Sunday. Chrysostom, for example, refers to reading Scripture "portion by portion" (Homily 9, John 1:9) and speaks explicitly of "the continual reading of the Holy Scriptures" (Homily 11, John 1:14).

The primary purpose of continuous reading of Scripture in worship and as a basis for preaching was largely catechetical—to instruct a worshiping community in the particulars of scripture and to increase familiarity with Scripture.[3] The scriptural story was the primary lens for worship in these services. As we have seen, as the liturgical year began to take shape in the history of the church, a different lens for reading scripture emerged, the selected reading with seasonal and thematic priorities (see chapters 1 and 2). A passage from one of Augustine's sermons describes the place of selected and continuous reading in worship:

> You remember, holy brethren, that the Gospel according to John, read in orderly course of lessons, is the subject on which we usually discourse: but because of the now intervening solemnity of the holy days, on which there must be certain lessons recited in the Church, which so come every year that they cannot be other than they are: the order which we had undertaken is of necessity for a little while intermitted, not wholly omitted. (Prologue to the Homilies on the First Epistle of John)

Recognizing the difference between the principle and practice of selected reading and of continuous (or semi-continuous) reading is pivotal for understanding the relationship between the incarnational and paschal cycles and the season of Ordinary Time. In the incarnational and paschal cycles, the Christ story determines how the lectionary is constructed, as texts are selected to proclaim the stories of Advent, birth, and the paschal mystery. By contrast, in Ordinary Time, reading through the biblical books assigned provides the structure for the season. The three lectionary years (A, B, and C) are built around a semi-continuous reading of the Synoptic Gospels (Matthew, Year A; Mark, Year B; Luke, Year C).

The *Lectionary for Mass*, the Roman Catholic lectionary that emerged out of Vatican II, embraced semi-continuous reading of the Gospel lesson in Ordinary Time, and of the second lesson, normally an Epistle but the first reading from the Hebrew Scripture was selected on the basis of the Gospel text, usually following a kind of typological or prophecy-fulfillment model. That meant that Hebrew Scripture did not stand on its own, but was given its meaning only as it related to the Gospel lesson. The Hebrew prophets were read not for what they said about Israel in their own day, for example, but for how they foreshadowed the ministry of Jesus.

The *Common Lectionary*, the forerunner of the RCL, followed this Roman Catholic practice, as do the traditional Episcopal and Lutheran lectionaries, so that the Jesus story as told in the Gospel assigned for a Sunday in Ordinary Time determines the selection of a lesson from Hebrew Scripture. This aspect of the *Common Lectionary* drew the most complaints from those Protestant churches that used it. Those churches that used the CL sensed that this approach to the OT denied the textual and theological integrity of the Hebrew canon and also severely restricted the type and range of OT texts that were available for public worship.[4] Correcting the way the OT texts were selected in Ordinary Time was the main motivator for revising the *Common Lectionary* and creating the *Revised Common Lectionary*.[5]

The RCL employs two different patterns for selecting the first (OT) lesson. For the Sundays between Epiphany and Lent, the RCL continues the pattern of the Roman lectionary (as well as the pattern in the Lutheran and Episcopal lectionaries) of choosing the OT passage for its close relation with the Gospel lesson.[6] For the Sundays after Pentecost, however, a sense of an overarching canonical narrative guides the selection of OT texts.[7] Individual Sunday lessons are not coordinated in order to illumine the Gospel text; instead the coordination occurs at the broader canonical level. Old Testament books are assigned to a particular cycle with an eye to what texts from Hebrew Scripture were significant theological and narrative resources for the Gospel writers. This intent is quite different from a typological or prophecy-fulfillment model. This way of coordinating Hebrew Scripture with the Gospels enables contemporary Christians to participate in a scriptural conversation similar to that in which early Christians participated instead of presenting Hebrew Scripture as subordinated to the readings from the NT.

In the Sundays after Pentecost, the books of the Pentateuch, important conversation partners for Matthew, provide most of the OT lessons for year A, the story of David and Wisdom texts provide the basis for Year B (to complement Mark), and readings from the Prophets, especially Jeremiah, receive the focus in Year C, reflecting the prophetic emphasis of Luke. The dominant pattern for the first lesson in Ordinary Time is semi-continuous, not selected reading. The signal contribution of this approach to the first lesson is that the lessons from Hebrew Scripture (Old Testament) become theological and pastoral resources in terms closer to their own. The portrait of God and of God's people in these lessons is not reduced to how it connects to or prepares for the story of Christ. Instead the breadth of its theological witness, its story of God and God's people, can be heard on its own.

Preaching in Ordinary Time

What difference does this pattern of text selection make to the preacher? For the majority of the Sundays of Ordinary Time, the preacher is presented with three semi-continuous readings—OT, Epistle, Gospel— that are not interconnected. As we have seen, in the incarnational and paschal cycles, the lessons are selected to go together, so that more than one lesson can and often should be preached to tell the story of the season. The three distinct semi-continuous cycles mean that for the majority of Sundays of Ordinary Time, the lessons do not go together and usually should not be preached together. The OT, Epistle, and Gospel provide three different perspectives on the story and life of faith. This distinction between lectionary cycles and seasons is often ignored in lectionary aids, so that the preacher is left confused about whether to coordinate the lessons in Ordinary Time.

The semi-continuous reading pattern creates opportunities for congregational exposure to a wider range of biblical texts than is possible in the incarnational and paschal cycles. In Ordinary Time, the preacher can place before his or her worshiping congregation large sections of the stories of the Hebrew Bible, as well as continuous readings from the Synoptic Gospels in narrative/chronological order. The Sundays of Ordinary Time also provide one of the few opportunities for a congregation to hear continuous readings from Pauline or other epistolary material (Year A, Romans, Philippians, 1 Thessalonians; Year B, 2 Corinthians, Ephesians, James, and Hebrews; Year C, Galatians, Colossians, 1 and 2 Timothy, 2 Thessalonians). The breadth and diversity of scripture move to the center of homiletical interests.

In the Sundays of Ordinary Time, the biblical texts themselves provide the main context for preaching, not the liturgical year. If in the incarnational and paschal cycles the liturgical calendar is the shaping context for lesson selection, in Ordinary Time something closer to a canonical context shapes lesson selection.[8] There is no overarching story such as Advent or Lent with which the lessons are placed into conversation. Rather, in the RCL, Ordinary Time is the "season" in which the congregation can place its life in the flow of the biblical stories and experience the intersections of the biblical texts and world with the contemporary world.

This shift from calendar to canon as the organizing principle for lesson selection carries with it a complementary shift in the lectionary preacher's sermon preparation. The charting that was outlined and modeled in chapters 5 and 6 cannot be undertaken in Ordinary Time, since there is no overarching seasonal narrative. The preacher is not looking for themes that tie the lessons to one another or that show the place of any given Sunday in the unfolding of the season. Instead, the effective lectionary preacher in Ordinary Time will take as his or her starting and continuing reference points the biblical texts themselves—their canonical contexts, their place in the flow of the biblical book from week to week, and so on. Rather than charting the season, the effective lectionary preacher is best served by *mapping the biblical books* that are being read throughout Ordinary Time.

Mapping Ordinary Time

Mapping the biblical books of Ordinary Time, like charting the season, will be most effective if the preacher is able to do this mapping at the beginning of Ordinary Time.[9] Given that the three lessons proceed on a semi-continuous basis throughout the Sundays after Pentecost, the initial mapping work that a preacher does will serve all the Sundays of Ordinary Time. In the model that follows, we will use Year B as an example.

First Step: Identify the Canonical Terrain

The first step for the lectionary preacher at Ordinary Time is to read through the lectionary listing of all the texts for the Sundays after Pentecost in order to get a sense of the canonical terrain that will be mapped. This is an essential first step, as it enables the preacher to see these Sundays whole. Ironically, the semi-continuous reading pattern of the lessons can lead the preacher to engage the Sundays after Pentecost a few weeks at a time, rather than reading initially for the whole season, since the lessons, like the weeks of the season, will simply proceed seriatim and therefore seem not to require planning. Yet just as the lectionary preacher needs a sense of the narrative of the liturgical seasons before crafting individual sermons for those seasons, the lectionary preacher in Ordinary Time needs a sense of the canonical terrain of the biblical books from which the lessons will be drawn. Even though the lectionary preacher is not going to chart the whole season, he or she nonetheless needs the foundation of a seasonal scriptural map. This holds true even for seasoned preachers who have preached through the three-year cycles many times before; one can have a selective memory about what is and is not designated as a lesson for Ordinary Time.

The easiest terrain to identify is that of the Gospel lessons, as each of the Synoptic Gospels has a year dedicated to it. Year B is Mark, yet a careful examination of the Gospel lessons slated for Year B show immediately why this first step is necessary. The Sundays after Pentecost begin with Mark 2:23–3:6 and conclude with John 18:33-37. Years A and C begin and end respectively with Matthew and Luke, so this first step has shown us that Year B varies from the common pattern of those two years. As one reads through the listing of all the Gospel lessons for Ordinary Time B, one finds another such variation from the semi-continuous reading of Mark. The Gospel lesson for the Sunday between July 10 and 16 inclusive is Mark 6:30-34, 53-56, but the next five Sundays in a row have a Gospel lesson from John 6. Mark will not return as the Gospel lesson until the Sunday between August 28 and September 3 inclusive. The lectionary preacher in Year B will need familiarity with both Mark and John.

The reason for the inclusion of non-Markan texts as Gospel lessons in Year B is quite pragmatic: as the shortest Gospel, Mark cannot fill all the Sundays of the church year on its own. Yet this pragmatic reason does not address why these particular Johannine texts were chosen to fill out the Markan year. Mapping the specifics of these variations will wait until step three of the mapping process, but the attention to the basic terrain has revealed a very important dimension of the Gospel lessons for Year B.

The basic canonical terrain for the first lesson (OT) is the story of David. The Sundays after Pentecost begin with a reading of 1 Samuel 3:1-10, (11-20), the call of Samuel.[10] The David story continues through David's death and instructions to Solomon (1 Kgs 2:10-12; 3:3-14) and concludes with Solomon's dedication of the Temple (1 Kgs 8). Year B is rounded out by two types of literature that have a canonical connection to the David story: Wisdom literature (since wisdom is traditionally associated with Solomon) and Ruth (for its place in the genealogy of David). The Wisdom texts do not offer a continuous reading of any single part of the wisdom tradition, but instead provide samples from across the tradition (Song of Songs, Proverbs, Esther, Job). Two lessons from 1 and 2 Samuel conclude Ordinary Time, selected for their connection with the eschatological themes with which Ordinary Time ends. Identifying the OT terrain suggests that the lectionary preacher will need to be familiar with the David story as told in Samuel-Kings and with the place of David and David traditions in the formation of the Hebrew canon.

The terrain of the Epistles is more straightforward than that of the Gospel or OT lessons. For the Sundays after Pentecost, Year B, the Epistle lessons read semi-continuously through 2 Corinthians (six lessons), Ephesians (seven lessons), James (five lessons), and Hebrews (six lessons). The last Sunday of Pentecost, Reign of Christ, concludes with a lesson from Revelation, fitting the eschatological impulse of the end of the year. Discovering just how continuous these readings are—that is, how much and what is eliminated—will wait for another step. The Epistle lessons for Year B are challenging for the preacher, as they range across four very different NT books, one universally recognized Pauline

Epistle (2 Corinthians) and three books of contested and unknown authorship and setting.

Second Step: Reading for Familiarity

Once the canonical terrain is identified, for the second step the preacher should forget about the lists of lectionary lessons and instead focus on the biblical books from which the lectionary texts have been selected. This step is crucial to effective preaching in Ordinary Time, and time spent with the biblical books early in the preaching season will reap benefits throughout Ordinary Time.

One of the genuine drawbacks with the lectionary, even in Ordinary Time with its pattern of semi-continuous reading, is the way that scripture is excerpted. The worshiping congregation rarely gets the sense of the flow and sweep of an entire biblical book because the texts tend to be selected on the "snippet principle."[11] The preacher will see the "snippet principle" very clearly when doing step one—note, for example, the way the death of David is excerpted. The lectionary selects 1 Kings 2:10-12; 3:3-14, a small part of the transition narrative that begins in 1 Kings 1. In order to preach effectively in Ordinary Time, the preacher must counterbalance the "snippet principle" by becoming familiar with the biblical books from which the lectionary passages are drawn and not merely familiarizing himself or herself with the lectionary passages. One of the contributions of the lessons of Ordinary Time to the worship life of congregations is that they enable the congregation to participate in a wider and deeper biblical conversation than is possible during the incarnational and paschal cycles. For that reason, the preacher cannot only study and prepare what is excerpted in the lectionary; during Ordinary Time it is incumbent upon him or her to become familiar with all the biblical books that provide the fabric for Year B. The canonical terrain that was identified in step one becomes the substance of step two.

Biblical commentaries are not necessary for this step, and, indeed, their use would actually interfere with accomplishing the goals of this step. In step two, the preacher is reading to increase and deepen his or her biblical facility and awareness. The preacher is not yet analyzing or assessing, but simply becoming acquainted with the array of texts that constitute the lessons for Ordinary Time. The benefits of this step will extend beyond Ordinary Time, as it facilitates the preacher's deepened and refined engagement with the biblical canon.

Our recommendation for this step is that the preacher read in their entirety each of the biblical books from which texts have been drawn for Ordinary Time, Year B. This reading will be most effective if each book is read through in one sitting, rather than read piecemeal. The preacher may also want to read the biblical books in a translation with which he or she is less familiar; for example, if the preacher normally uses the NIV, read the NRSV for this step and vice versa. A new translation will enable the preacher to notice things that a familiar translation often masks. This step is the backbone around which the entire season's lectionary preaching will be constructed. Practically, to skip this step will simply mean playing catch-up later in the season.

The variety of biblical texts in Ordinary Time ensures that the preacher who completes this step each year for each lectionary cycle will stay familiar with a wide range of biblical materials. This familiarity will ensure that the preacher will be able to take advantage of the catechetical dimension of Ordinary Time to increase a congregation's biblical literacy and fluency. At the end of this chapter we will discuss what parts of the Bible are not represented in the lectionary, especially in Ordinary Time, and what that suggests for a biblically-informed preaching ministry.

Third Step: Constructing the Lectionary Map

The next step is for the preacher to create three maps of the lessons in Ordinary Time: one map for each of the three main lessons.[12] Critical to the construction of these maps is to identify the particular lessons from a given biblical book that are included in the lectionary and to note those parts of the text that are excluded, omitted, or ignored.

The Gospel Map

The Gospel map is the easiest place to begin, since it involves only one NT book (although as we have seen, Mark also includes several readings from the Gospel of John which will need to be mapped). The semi-continuous reading of the Gospel actually begins with the Sundays after Epiphany, so in order to map fully the congregation's experience of the Markan story, the preacher needs to look at those Sundays as well.[13]

Map of Mark in the Sundays after the Epiphany[14]

Sunday	Gospel Reading	Break in Sequence
First Sunday after the Epiphany	Mark 1:4-11	**(Mark 1:1-3)**
Second Sunday	**John 1:43-51**	**Mark 1:12-13**
Third Sunday	Mark 1:14-20	
Fourth Sunday	Mark 1:21-28	
Fifth Sunday	Mark 1:29-39	
Sixth Sunday (Proper 1)	Mark 1:40-45	
Seventh Sunday (Proper 2)	Mark 2:1-12	
Eighth Sunday (Proper 3)	Mark 2:13-22	
Ninth Sunday (Proper 4)	Mark 2:23–3:6	

This map reveals several items of interest and help to the preacher. First, one sees again that a reading from John is intercalated into the readings from Mark. A reading from the Gospel of John occurs on the Second Sunday after Epiphany in all three lectionary cycles. One of the emphases of John is Jesus' revelation (epiphany) to the world, and the selection of this lesson acknowledges that role. Second, the first and second Sundays after the Epiphany come closest to having a seasonal theme of any of the Sundays in this part of Ordinary Time, as they always tell the story of Jesus' baptism and an epiphany narrative from John. As we have noted, Ordinary Time ends thematically (with an emphasis on eschatology and the Reign of Christ) and now we see that it begins thematically as well. The semi-continuous reading of Mark begins in earnest on the Third Sunday after Epiphany. Third, two units of Mark 1–2 are omitted in these Sundays—Mark 1:1-3, the opening verses of the Gospel, and Mark 2:12-13, the very brief Markan temptation narrative. These two passages have been read earlier in the liturgical year—Mark 1:1-8 is the lesson for Advent 2, B, and the temptation narrative is the traditional lesson for the

First Sunday in Lent. We will discuss below the relationship of readings in Ordinary Time to Markan readings in liturgical seasons.

Map of Mark for the Sundays after Pentecost

Sunday	Gospel Reading	Break in Sequence
Trinity Sunday (First Sunday after Pentecost)[15]	**John 3:1-17**	
Ninth Sunday of Ordinary Time (Proper 4)[16]	Mark 2:23–3:6	
Tenth Sunday	Mark 3:20-35	**Mark 3:7-19**
Eleventh Sunday	Mark 4:26-34	**Mark 4:1-25**
Twelfth Sunday	Mark 4:35-41	
Thirteenth Sunday	Mark 5:21-43	**Mark 5:1-20**
Fourteenth Sunday	Mark 6:1-13	
Fifteenth Sunday	Mark 6:14-29	
Sixteenth Sunday	Mark 6:30-34, 53-56	**Mark 6:35-52**
Seventeenth Sunday	**John 6:1-21**	
Eighteenth Sunday	**John 6:24-35**	John 6:22-23
Nineteenth Sunday	**John 6:35, 41-51**	John 6:36-40
Twentieth Sunday	**John 6:51-58**	
Twenty-first Sunday	**John 6:56-69**	
Twenty-second Sunday	Mark 7:1-8, 14-15, 21-23	**Mark 7:9-13, 17-23**
Twenty-third Sunday	Mark 7:24-37	
Twenty-fourth Sunday	Mark 8:27-38	**Mark 8:1-26**
Twenty-fifth Sunday	Mark 9:30-37	**Mark 9:1-29**

Twenty-sixth Sunday	Mark 9:38-50	
Twenty-seventh Sunday	Mark 10:2-16	**Mark 10:1**
Twenty-eighth Sunday	Mark 10:17-31	
Twenty-ninth Sunday	Mark 10:35-45	**Mark 10:32-34**
Thirtieth Sunday	Mark 10:46-52	
Thirty-first Sunday	Mark 12:28-34	**Mark 11,** **Mark 12:1-27**
Thirty-second Sunday	Mark 12:38-44	**Mark 12:35-37**
Thirty-third Sunday	Mark 13:1-8	
Thirty-fourth Sunday (Proper 29)	**John 18:33-37**	

The mapping above helps to orient the preacher to the use of Mark in Ordinary Time. We will provide a sample of some of the ways that mapping increases the preacher's fluency with the larger Markan narrative and the particularities of Mark's use in the lectionary. This fluency in turn provides a solid foundation when the preacher turns to the work of individual sermon preparation.

1. Flow of the Gospel Narrative

The first two chapters of Mark are included in the lectionary readings almost in their entirety. After the contours of the Jesus story are established, however, the map shows the way that the lectionary begins to pick and choose Markan stories. The narrative/chronological order of the lessons is maintained as part of the semi-continuous reading—no story is read out of narrative sequence—but the story is abbreviated. An examination of a few of the units that are omitted (the "Break in Sequence" column in the map) show a range of factors in play.

a. The first break in the narrative sequence (with the exception of the omission of the temptation narrative) occurs at Mark 3:7. The RCL omits Mark 3:7-12, a type of passage commonly referred to as a "Markan summary," in which the Gospel writer gives a summary presentation of the teaching and healing ministry of Jesus. Close reading of the map shows that summary passages are regularly omitted from the lectionary readings (for example, Mark 10:1). The omission of the summaries suggests an emphasis in the lectionary on the immediacy of the individual stories that are being read, and not on providing an overview or retrospective of Jesus' ministry. This emphasis on immediacy is a clue to the preacher on how to use Mark.

b. The RCL gives priority to stories over parts of the gospel that contain teachings. The units of Mark that are omitted in the RCL (Mark 4:1-25; 7:9-13, 17-23; Mark 12:1-27; Mark 12:35-37) are all teaching units. In addition, in the sections from Mark 7 and Mark 12 that are omitted, the teachings have to do with interpretation of Jewish cultic practice and legal traditions. Mark 4:1-25 introduces Jesus' parables in Mark; a few of the parables are included but not the parable that frames this chapter, the parable of the sower.

c. The RCL eliminates repetition in its selection of texts. Mark contains two miraculous feedings, Mark 6 and Mark 8. The Mark 6 story is included in the RCL; the Mark 8:1-10 story is omitted. Similarly, there are two stories of the healing of blind men in Mark, Mark 8:22-26 and 10:46-52; the RCL omits the first story. Jesus predicts his passion three times in Mark (8:31-33; 9:30-32; 10:32-34). The RCL includes the first two, but omits the third.

Again, there are quite pragmatic reasons for these decisions—there are a limited number of Sundays in Ordinary Time. Essentially, each Gospel has to be read through in thirty-four weeks; something has to be omitted. But these repetitions are an important part of the way the central section of Mark is structured. The central section is framed by the two sight miracles, suggesting a gradual move from blindness to sight, and the three Passion predictions communicate a similar movement both in the disciples' comprehension and in Jesus' movement toward his death. By giving preference to a strict linear progression and eliminating repetitions, the RCL tells a slightly different Markan story than the one the Gospel itself tells. Because the preacher has mapped both what is included and what is omitted from the RCL, he or she is better prepared to attend to the full Markan picture.

It is also important to remember that the Sunday lectionary is only one form of lectionary use for any given year. There is also a daily lectionary, and in the daily lectionary, most of these omissions are restored. For example, the daily lectionary reads Mark 4 in its entirety. Nonetheless, since most members of a worshiping congregation depend on the Sunday lectionary for their Scripture and do not use a daily lectionary, these omissions need to be noted by the preacher as part of preaching preparation.

Yet not all omissions have to do only with economy of storytelling or fitting the Gospel into the Sundays of the year. We have noted above that some of the teaching material that is eliminated from Mark 7 and 12 is material that focuses specifically on Jewish cultic practice and legal traditions. These were questions that were of immediate importance for Jesus' audience and for the first readers of the Gospel but that are not seen as having the same relevance for contemporary Christians, the majority of whom are Gentile, not Jewish, in religious heritage. Yet to eliminate these texts from the lectionary is to remove an important part of the Christian heritage and story from the preaching life of the church.

We noted that the lectionary prefers story texts to teaching texts, but there is one type of story in Mark that is consistently omitted from the lessons—stories in which Jesus exorcises a demon and so effects a healing. This is an important part of Jesus' ministry in Mark, and yet such stories are absent from the readings in Ordinary Time. One of Mark's most elaborate narratives, the healing of the Gerasene demoniac (5:1-20), is absent from the readings in the RCL. Talk of demon possession and personified evil is alien to many contemporary worldviews, but it was a vital part of the biblical world and its absence in the lectionary excuses the lectionary preacher from having to struggle with these questions and impoverishes our preaching.

2. Relationship of Readings in Ordinary Time to Markan Readings in the Liturgical Seasons

We have already noted that the opening verses of Mark are not read in Ordinary Time because they have been read in Advent, and that the temptation narrative (Mark 1:12-13) is omitted in Ordinary Time because it is read during Lent. Similarly, Mark 11 is omitted in Ordinary Time, because its central stories—the triumphal entry and the cleansing of the Temple—belong to the paschal cycle. And the last lesson from Mark in Ordinary Time is Mark 13:1-8, the beginning of the "Little Apocalypse." More of that apocalyptic text begins Year B (Advent 1, Mark 13:24-37). The Markan Passion Narrative (Mark 14:1–15:47) is the Gospel lesson for the Sixth Sunday in Lent, Year B, and Mark 16:1-8, the empty tomb narrative, is the Gospel lesson for Easter Sunday.

The Markan readings in other parts of the liturgical year fill out the Gospel portrait and ensure that the congregation will have lived the Markan story quite extensively in Year B. Assuming that the preacher followed the lectionary from Advent through Pentecost, the congregation's familiarity with the sections of Mark that they have already read provides a context for the use of Mark in Ordinary Time. It is important to note, however, that the omission of these lessons in Ordinary Time, particularly the temptation, the triumphal entry, and the cleansing of the Temple, leave significant gaps in the flow of the Markan story. The selective use of some Markan lessons, and the semi-continuous reading of others, can create an imbalance to which the preacher will need to attend.

3. Length and Division of the Lessons

An examination of the mapping of Mark shows great variety in the length of lessons. For the lessons that occur early in the year (the Sundays after the Epiphany), Mark 1 and 2 are read in sequence and divided into passages of similar length. This provides the congregation with a smooth introduction to the continuous reading of Mark in worship. As Ordinary Time progresses, however, the lessons become of increasingly varied length. The lesson for the Thirteenth Sunday after Pentecost, for example, is over twenty verses long (Mark 5:21-43), whereas the lesson for the Thirty-first Sunday after Pentecost is only seven verses long (Mark 12:28-34). The lessons for the Sixteenth Sunday (Mark 6:30-34, 53-56) and for the Twenty-second Sunday (Mark 7:1-8, 14-25, 21-23) consist of excerpts from a chapter, instead of a sustained unit of text. The variety in length is a challenge for the preacher and requires a variety of homiletical strategies. The longer lessons can require that the preacher take the long view, whereas the very short lessons necessitate a different kind of textual and homiletical engagement.

The length of the lessons is often determined by the RCL's sense of what constitutes a textual unit. Sometimes a lesson is unusually long because the story it contains is long; that is the case with Mark 5:21-43, the double healing story of the girl restored to life and the woman with the hemorrhage. The two healing stories are intertwined in Mark's narrative, and the unit cannot be abbreviated without damage to the text. It can be complicated for the preacher to negotiate these two stories, but Mark has told them in a way that requires this negotiation. Sometimes, however, the RCL combines narrative units in ways that complicate the preaching task. Mark 3:20-35 are consecutive verses in Mark, yet these verses contain several discrete units: the question of whether Jesus is demon possessed and the assorted teachings that follow (vv. 20-27), a teaching on the sin against the Holy Spirit (vv. 28-30), and a story about who is Jesus' family (vv. 31-35). To try to preach all of these units in one sermon is a formidable task. Mapping the Markan lessons enables the preacher to anchor such complex lessons more effectively in the over-arching Markan narrative.

4. Mark 6 and John 6

The intercalation of John 6 into the semi-continuous reading of Mark is quite apparent in the mapping. For five weeks, an almost continuous reading of John 6 interrupts the flow of Mark. As the map shows, the lessons are arranged in such a way that the feeding of the 5000 in John 6 substitutes for this story in Mark 6. Interestingly, the lesson from Mark 6 that begins the sequence on the feeding miracle contains the setup for the feeding miracle (6:30-34) and a summary of Jesus' ministry up through the point of the feeding (6:53-56), but not the miracle itself. Mark serves as the frame into which the Johannine narrative is placed, but is not allowed to tell its own story. The RCL Gospel story makes a dramatic shift for five weeks, as Mark disappears.

The feeding of the five thousand in John is one of the richest narratives in that Gospel. The first reading from John in this sequence narrates both the feeding miracle and Jesus' walking on water (Mark's version of this story is one of the parts of Mark that is omitted in the RCL). The next four weeks contain sections of the Bread of Life discourse from John 6, in which John interprets the feeding miracle and the walking on water as acts of Jesus' self-revelation to the world. These texts are central to the narrative and theological unfolding of the story of Jesus in John, and without their inclusion in this part of Year B, the church would never hear these pivotal parts of John in worship. Yet their inclusion in Year B also provides the preacher with an unusual challenge because he or she needs to be well-versed in John as well as in Mark. Their inclusion also makes visible the ways in which the lessons of the RCL, even in Ordinary Time, are not simply proceeding sequentially through biblical texts but are constructing their own particular story. John's voice is positioned explicitly to supplement and comment on Mark in a way that does not occur in the NT itself.

The Map of the First Lessons and Epistle Lessons

The first lessons (OT) and Epistle lessons also need to be mapped in order to position the preacher to best advantage as he or she approaches preaching in Ordinary Time. Obviously, because the OT and Epistle lessons try to cover a wider range of biblical material than the Gospel lessons do, the maps of these lessons will look different. There will be more breaks in sequence because the OT and epistolary literature are read even more semi-continuously than the Gospel is. The mapping of the first and second lessons will entail a series of distinct maps—to reflect the range of canonical materials—rather than one continuous map. Finally, the mapping of the first lessons can begin only with the Sundays after Pentecost, since for the Sundays after the Epiphany, selected reading, not continuous reading, is used for the OT lessons; those lessons are selected to illumine or complement the Gospel lesson. For the purposes of this chapter, we will map the opening segment of the OT lessons and the Epistle lessons for the same Sundays.

Map of the First Lesson for the Sundays after Pentecost[17]

Sunday	OT Lesson	Break in Sequence
Ninth Sunday of Ordinary Time (Proper 4)	1 Samuel 3:1-10, (11-20)	(1 Samuel 1 and 2)
Tenth Sunday	1 Samuel 8:4-11, (12-15), 16-20; (11:14-15)	1 Samuel 3; 4; 5; 6; 7; 8:1-3; 9; 10; 11:1-13
Eleventh Sunday	1 Samuel 15:34–16:13	1 Samuel 12; 13; 14; 15:1-33
Twelfth Sunday	1 Samuel 17: (1a, 4-11, 19-23), 32-49 or 1 Samuel 17:57-18:5, 10-16	1 Samuel 16:14-23; [1 Samuel 17: (1a, 4-11, 19-23), 32-49 or 1 Samuel 17:57–18:5, 10-16]

Thirteenth Sunday	2 Samuel 1:1, 17-27	**1 Samuel 18:17–31:13; 2 Samuel 1:2-16**
Fourteenth Sunday	2 Samuel 5:1-5, 9-10	**2 Samuel 2–4; 5:6-8**
Fifteenth Sunday	2 Samuel 6:1-5, 12b-19	**2 Samuel 6:6-12a**
Sixteenth Sunday	2 Samuel 7:1-14a	**2 Samuel 6:20-23**
Seventeenth Sunday	2 Samuel 11:1-15	**2 Samuel 8–10**
Eighteenth Sunday	2 Samuel 11:26–12:13a	**2 Samuel 11:16-25**
Nineteenth Sunday	2 Samuel 18:5-9, 15, 31-33	**2 Samuel 12:13b–18:4; 18:10-14, 16-30**
Twentieth Sunday	1 Kings 2:10-12; 3:3-14	**2 Samuel 19–24; 1 Kings 1:1–2:9; 2:13–3:9**
Twenty-first Sunday	1 Kings 8:1, 6, 10-11, 22-30, 41-43	**1 Kings 3:15–7:51**

The number of breaks in sequence in the OT lessons reinforces why the mapping needs to be the third step. The preacher first must be acquainted with the books of Samuel in their entirety in order to recognize how the story has been excerpted for the lectionary. We will offer a few samples of what can be learned from this map that will assist the lectionary preacher.

Even a cursory glance at the map reveals that the OT lessons are much more excerpted than are the Gospel lessons. As with the Gospel lesson, there is a pragmatic reason for much of this excerpting: 1 and 2 Samuel contain fifty-seven chapters, so these books must be abbreviated to fit the contours of Ordinary Time. This abbreviation is evident not only in the large blocks of narrative material that are simply omitted but also in the way that individual lessons are excerpted. The RCL attempts to provide the gist of individual stories without all of the exegetical details.

Yet once the preacher has recognized this pragmatic dimension of the text selection, he or she must then read carefully to see what parts of 1 and 2 Samuel are included and what are omitted in order to understand the narrative arc of these lessons. The books of Samuel have been streamlined to tell one story—the story of David. The role of other central figures of 1 Samuel—Samuel, Saul, and Jonathan— are reduced to the part they play in the David story or eliminated altogether. Stories about women also are almost completely omitted. The mapping shows that the opening chapters of Samuel that tell of Samuel's birth and childhood are not included in Ordinary Time. These chapters contain Hannah's song (2 Sam 2:1-10), a song on which the Magnificat of Mary (Luke 1:46-55) is modeled, but because these chapters focus on Samuel's story, not David's, they are omitted at this point.[18]

The lessons for the Ninth through Eleventh Sundays show that only the parts of Samuel's story that focus on his role in establishing the monarchy and anointing David for the role of king are included in Ordinary Time (note the large blocks of material that are omitted). Saul and Jonathan are essentially invisible in the lectionary readings because to tell their story would distract from the focus on David. It is important for the preacher to recognize that these lessons tell the story of King David; they do not tell the story of ancient Israel of which David was a part.

In addition, the lessons tell the David story quite selectively. If the preacher compares the omitted portions of 1 and 2 Samuel with what is included in the lectionary, he or she will notice that with two exceptions, the lessons tell the story of David's greatness without narrating any of the political and military acts that accomplished his rise to power. David is essentially de-historicized in these readings—little of the violence or intrigue that marked his reign belongs to the lectionary's storytelling.

The two exceptions are found in the last readings from 2 Samuel: the story of David and Bathsheba (the Seventeenth and Eighteenth Sundays) and the death of Absalom (the Nineteenth Sunday). On these Sundays, David the man, rather than simply David the king, enters the lectionary's storytelling.

This is particularly the case with the readings from 2 Samuel 18. Even in the abbreviated form that the lectionary suggests, the death of Absalom is one of the most pathos-filled stories in all of Scripture. Here, at the end of the David story, the full measure of the man is available for the worshiping congregation.

144

Map of the Epistle Lesson for the Sundays after Pentecost[19]

Sunday	Epistle Lesson	Break in Sequence
Ninth Sunday of Ordinary Time (Proper 4)	2 Corinthians 4:5-12	**(2 Corinthians 1:1-17; 2; 3:7-18)**
Tenth Sunday	2 Corinthians 4:13–5:1	
Eleventh Sunday	2 Corinthians 5:6-10, 11-13, 14-17	**2 Corinthians 5:2-5**
Twelfth Sunday	2 Corinthians 6:1-13	**2 Corinthians 5:18-21**
Thirteenth Sunday	2 Corinthians 8:7-15	**2 Corinthians 6:14–8:6**
Fourteenth Sunday	2 Corinthians 12:2-10	**2 Corinthians 8:16– 12:1; (2 Corinthians 12:11–13:13)**
Fifteenth Sunday	Ephesians 1:3-14	**Ephesians 1:1-2**
Sixteenth Sunday	Ephesians 2:11-22	**Ephesians 1:15–2:10**
Seventeenth Sunday	Ephesians 3:14-21	**Ephesians 3:1-10**
Eighteenth Sunday	Ephesians 4:1-16	
Nineteenth Sunday	Ephesians 4:25–5:2	**Ephesians 4:17-24**
Twentieth Sunday	Ephesians 5:15-20	**Ephesians 5:3-14**
Twenty-first Sunday	Ephesians 6:10-20	**Ephesians 5:21–6:9; 6:21-24**

Again, the mapping makes clear what is included and what is omitted in the Epistle lessons. A quick glance at the mappings indicates that there are a few weeks where the lessons are read continuously with no breaks, and that often only short passages are omitted. As with the Gospel and OT lessons, some of the omissions are pragmatic. The lessons are abbreviated and compressed in order to give a fair flavor of the theological voice and perspectives of a given book, yet still cover a wide range of epistolary material. Remember that lessons from four different books comprise the Epistle lessons for the Sundays after Pentecost.

A quick survey of the mapping of Ephesians, however, also gives a good sense of some of the exegetically, theologically, and pastorally substantive issues that the abbreviations surface for the preacher. The opening and closing verses of Ephesians are eliminated from the lessons: Ephesians 1:1-2 and 6:21-23. These verses are the greeting and closing of the letter, so that on the one hand, one could say that nothing of theological substance is omitted. Yet, on the other hand, these opening and closing verses are the only part of Ephesians that explicitly engage the epistolary form. Without them, the contemporary congregation misses the dimension of Paul as letter writer and does not get to experience this literary form that was so important to the ministry of the early church. Other Christians first received and read this letter, and when the epistolary frame is removed, the immediacy of this form of pastoral communication and the sense of both continuity and discontinuity between original and contemporary readers is lost. The preacher must find ways to reclaim these aspects of the letter when preaching the Ephesians lessons.

The omissions also eliminate one of Ephesians' most difficult passages from the lessons for Ordinary Time—Ephesians 5:21–6:6, the "household codes" that outline and prescribe proper relations within the Christian household. Most preachers are relieved that this text is not part of the lectionary, as the household codes preserve the values of the social and cultural world of the first-century and are offensive to many contemporary Christians. They appear to prescribe subservient roles for women and to sanction slavery, to name two problems. Yet the omission of this text from the lectionary does not really solve the problem of the tensions between the first-century world and the twenty-first-century world. In fact, because this text is removed from the preaching and worship life of the congregation, contemporary pastors and their communities can avoid negotiating some of the harder questions about the authority of Scripture and the relevance of first-century social teachings for a very different social world. The RCL often removes difficult texts from the lectionary,[20] and the lectionary preacher needs to be attuned to what this means for the theological and spiritual development of his or her congregation.

All three steps of this mapping have been done simply with the Bible and the lectionary lists of texts. No other tools are necessary, as at this point, the preacher's goal is to get as secure a sense as possible of the big picture out of which the lectionary texts are drawn. After these three steps are completed, the preacher is positioned to begin to engage other resources—for example, to read commentaries or selected books on larger issues in Mark, 1 and 2 Samuel, and Ephesians in order to refresh one's knowledge of the larger historical, literary, and theological issues that inform these biblical books and their interpretation. This kind of reading will apply across all six months of Ordinary Time and should not be done only for individual sermons. Rather, becoming fluent with the interpretive issues surrounding the biblical books read in Ordinary Time will reap dividends throughout Ordinary Time and will reduce the work required for each individual sermon. The preacher will have in place the foundation on which to build individual sermons as each week requires.

Preaching Strategies for Ordinary Time

1. Independent Lessons

When all three sequences of lessons are mapped, the rich array of texts at the preacher's disposal becomes apparent. Because the lessons for Ordinary Time, unlike the lessons in the incarnational and paschal cycles, are not coordinated with one another for each Sunday, what the preacher actually has in Ordinary Time is three independent sequences of texts from which to build his or her preaching ministry. The independence of the lessons is the key to any preaching strategy for Ordinary Time.

It can require considerable discipline to resist the urge to find a theme that connects one or more of the lessons during Ordinary Time, especially for the lectionary preacher who is used to looking for and finding connections in the other seasons of the year. Building on the mapping described above, we now provide thumbnail sketches of just a few passages, like those in step one of the charting exercise described in chapters 5 and 6. These thumbnail sketches make visible why looking for common themes is not a good preaching strategy for Ordinary Time.

Sunday	First Lesson	Epistle Lesson	Gospel Lesson
Ninth Sunday	1 Samuel 3:1-10, (11-20): The call of the young boy Samuel.	2 Corinthians 4:5-12: Paul's theology of ministry—God's power is made manifest in Paul's weakness and tribulations.	Mark 2:23–3:6: Two Sabbath controversy stories—plucking grain and healing on the Sabbath both constitute work.
Tenth Sunday	1 Samuel 8:4-11, (12-15), 16-20; (11:14-15): Israel demands a king to rule over them (instead of judges), even though the Lord is their own true king.	2 Corinthians 4:13–5:1: Paul's theology of ministry—The risen Jesus is the source of life. Paul knows that his suffering is for the greater glory of God's grace.	Mark 3:20-35: Several discrete teaching units—a house divided against itself; the sin against the Holy Spirit; "Who are my mother and my brothers?"
Eleventh Sunday	1 Samuel 15:34–16:13: Samuel discovers the young shepherd David and anoints him king.	2 Corinthians 5:6-10, (11-13), 14-17: Paul's ministry is grounded in the love of Christ. Christ's death and resurrection have ushered in a new creation.	Mark 4:26-34:Two parables of the kingdom—the scattered seed and the mustard seed.

In the incarnational and paschal cycles, the chart of thumbnail sketches is designed to be read horizontally (that is, from first lesson to second lesson to the Gospel lesson). A horizontal reading establishes the common theological and pastoral threads and themes. The above chart makes clear, however, that it is not possible to read the lessons "horizontally" in Ordinary Time, and indeed, such a way of reading usually undermines the integrity of the lessons. Israel's demand for a king (Tenth Sunday of Ordinary Time) has no thematic connection to Paul's theology of ministry, which in turn has no connection to the teachings of Mark 3. Instead, the connections need to be sought vertically—that is, the OT lesson for one Sunday should be read in conversation with the OT lesson for the Sundays that precede and follow it, not with the other lessons of the day.

Because of the independence of the appointed lessons, Ordinary Time provides the opportunity to tell the story of faith in much broader and diverse perspectives than is the case in the incarnational and paschal cycles. To look for the one thread that unites the lessons in Ordinary Time is to undercut this diversity because one ends up manufacturing themes that distort all the lessons. The lessons from 1 Samuel present one story of what it means to be God's people and to struggle to be faithful and to build community, and Paul's second letter to the Corinthians tells quite a different story about the religious life. Each of these stories has something to offer the worshiping community, but that offer will only be heard if each of the lessons is allowed to speak in its own voice and not forced into a conversation with the other lessons assigned for the day.

In essence, the RCL provides the preacher with three distinct cycles of texts. Since the preacher will not be able to preach all of the lessons provided in Ordinary Time in any single year, the RCL can be seen as providing the preacher with a nine-year cycle of texts.[21] To think of the lessons as containing enough texts for a nine-year cycle helps to illustrate the richness of biblical resources that the RCL makes available to the preacher and through him or her, to the worshiping congregation.

2. Lessons in Sequence

A synonym for Ordinary Time is counted time. This means, as we noted earlier, that the major organizing principle for Ordinary Time is simply the regular succession of Sundays. Week after week passes in the community's life, punctuated by the regular weekly celebration of the Lord's Day. The passing of time—and the record of the passing of time (for example, each week the church bulletin records where in the count of Ordinary Time the community stands)—are the character of this season. In this way, ordinary as "counted" is also synonymous with ordinary as "commonplace," because there is nothing special about the passing of time. Rather, the weeks of Ordinary Time enable the community to count the regular movement of its life with God and with one another in the world.

The semi-continuous reading practice of Ordinary Time communicates this regular passing of time—the lessons move in an orderly fashion through the biblical books appointed for this time of year. The preacher needs to select lessons for preaching in a way that communicates this regular, continuous movement of time. The mapping exercise is important here because it enables the preacher to see the big picture of each of the three lessons and so conceive of sermon series that respect the continuous reading practice of Ordinary Time. That means it does not make sense for the preacher to jump weekly from lesson to lesson—that is, preach a lesson from 1 Samuel one week, a lesson from 2 Corinthians the next, Mark the week after that. To follow such a pattern will not help a congregation increase their biblical fluency, because they will hear a series of unrelated sermons. Instead, the congregation is best served if the preacher follows the arc of the lessons to construct his or her sermons on a semi-continuous pattern. For Year B, for example, the preacher could begin the Sundays after Pentecost with a series of sermons on David, using the lessons from 1 and 2 Samuel; then turn to a series of sermons on Mark; then to a series of sermons on James; a series on Ruth, and so on. If the preacher constructs sermons for Ordinary Time in this way, he or she will provide the congregation with enough readings in succession from a particular book that the congregation will begin to hear the theological particulars of that biblical witness.

3. Discovery of the Breadth and Diversity of the Biblical Material

To undertake to explore coherent lesson blocks in the sermon will also move the preacher away from preaching only texts with which he or she is already familiar, which in most instances translates into the fallback position of preaching the Gospel lesson every week.[22] To preach only lessons from the Synoptic Gospels communicates that the only part of the Bible that is necessary for Christian life and faith is stories about Jesus, even though the breadth and depth of the canon witnesses otherwise. Whereas the preacher may not consciously intend to communicate this, such a narrowing of the biblical conversation is the effect of nurturing a congregation's faith and witness only with Gospel lessons. The preacher's own spiritual nurturing suffers as well, because he or she misses the opportunity to explore the breadth of the biblical witness and discover afresh the dynamism of the Christian faith.

At the heart of the Christian faith is the proclamation that for the Christian community, God is known decisively in Jesus Christ, but the early Christians were able to recognize God in Christ because of what they already knew and had experienced of God through the stories of God in the Hebrew Scriptures. Dietrich Bonhoeffer, who offered powerful and compelling Christian witness against the horrors of Nazi Germany, spoke of the ways in which the Christian faith was severely truncated without the witness of the Old Testament. For Bonhoeffer, preaching the Old Testament was one way to ensure that Christian proclamation was grounded in the events of this world.[23] The books of the Old Testament cover the sweep of history in a way that the New Testament, recording the faithful witness of just a few decades of religious life, cannot. The Old Testament enables the worshiping community to engage the stories of real communities who tried to live faithfully within the realities of domestic and political life. The Old Testament contains examples of people who both succeed and fail in their efforts to live in right relationship with God and with one another. To proclaim the presence and good news of God in all those struggles is to come closer to the ways that contemporary peoples struggle to be at one with God's hopes for the world.

Perhaps most important, when the preacher neglects the OT as a resource for preaching, he or she severely limits the ways in which God can be known and will be present for the worshiping community. Paul articulates this powerfully when he speaks of the continuum between the God of Abraham and the God who is revealed in the death and resurrection of Jesus. The God in whom Abraham believed is the God "who gives life to the dead and calls into existence the things that do not exist" (Rom 4:17). Paul and other early Christians were able to speak powerfully about the revelation of God in Jesus because their scriptures had already revealed to them the life-giving powers of God. In the creation stories, the stories of barren women giving birth, the exodus journey from slavery to freedom, the journey from exile to restoration—all of these stories testified to God's power of life over death. The resurrection belongs to this deep and rich story of God and God's will and hope for God's creation. A congregation's experience of God and of God's place in their lives and their world needs to be sustained and formed by the proclamation of the OT.

A church's experience of the preached Word of God also is limited when the epistolary literature is not a regular part of preaching. Given the proportion of sermons that are preached on the Gospel lessons, one would think that the Gospels are the dominant literary form in the NT, but of course they are not. There are four canonical Gospels compared to twenty-one Epistles, and to omit the Epistles from preaching is to limit the picture of Christian proclamation and witness. Not only do Epistles testify to the ways and places in which Christianity spread in the first century, but perhaps more important for contemporary communities of faith, they provide glimpses into the particularities of how early Christian communities tried to define the new life and faith to which they were called. The Epistles witness to very pragmatic struggles of these early communities—how do we order worship, how do we define community membership, what behaviors are detrimental to community life—as well as to the theological questions that animated and resolved these struggles. The Epistles remind us that part of Christian faith is to ask about the stuff of religious life—for example, what is reconciliation, what is hope, what is faith? Early Christians and their leaders thought and talked intensely and with great seriousness about the meaning of their faith. To include the Epistles as a regular part of the preaching and worship life of a congregation creates new possibilities for similar conversations in contemporary communities.

To preach from the Epistles also challenges a preacher to stretch his or her own preaching style. Preachers tend to gravitate toward the stories of the Bible as the mainstay of preaching, and to preach nonnarrative texts like Paul (and the OT prophets and Wisdom literature) creates opportunities for the preacher to try new ways to proclaim the good news of God. Not all of life can be captured in stories, and the situational immediacy and theological directness of Paul can model new pastoral and homiletical directions.[24]

To Preach or Not to Preach: Leaving the Lectionary in Ordinary Time

In the incarnational and paschal cycles, where liturgical time and the lectionary texts are so interdependent and mutually informed, the lessons appointed in the RCL are more than simply scriptural lessons. As we have seen, they tell a coherent narrative of the Christ story and so guide the congregation on its journey from Advent through Pentecost. Because that narrative and liturgical cohesion is not intrinsic to the lessons of Ordinary Time, for preachers in traditions that do not mandate lectionary use for Sunday worship, Ordinary Time can provide the opportunity to leave the lectionary occasionally and use other biblical texts for preaching. What can guide the preacher in making the decision to vary from the lectionary and in selecting alternative texts?

This book has highlighted many strengths of the lectionary, but there also are some limitations. Some of these have been mentioned in this chapter—unusual division of passages, a tendency to avoid difficult texts (for example, texts of violence, judgment, culturally determined social practices), the near absence of stories about women. In addition, even though the three years of lessons for Ordinary Time do cover a vast amount of scripture, they do not do justice to the full range and diversity of biblical texts. The major narrative cycles of the OT lessons in Year A (Pentateuch) and Year B (1 and 2 Samuel), for example, tend to focus on the "great men" of those cycles (Abraham, Jacob, Moses, David) and not on the fullness of the stories in which those men are embedded. In all three years of the lectionary, only one lesson from Leviticus appears (Lev 19:1-2, 9-18) and a sampling of texts from Numbers and Deuteronomy. Joshua and Judges are almost invisible in the lectionary, and there are no texts from the Chronicler's version of the David story. The prophets are heavily weighted toward Isaiah and Jeremiah. For the NT, the Gospel of John occurs mainly in the liturgical cycles and rarely in Ordinary Time. This makes it difficult for congregations to engage in the theological voice and vision of John as a regular part of their worship. Acts is represented only in the seven Sundays of Easter and the only texts from Revelation are those that depict scenes of heavenly worship or celebrate the New Jerusalem. The heart of that important book is completely absent from the lectionary.

If the preacher takes seriously that Ordinary Time provides the opportunity to present his or her congregation with the breadth and depth of the biblical witness, then that very commitment can guide the preacher in varying some of the lessons prescribed by the RCL. Since the lectionary cycles repeat every three years, the regular lectionary preacher can use this repetition to insert even more texts into a congregation's repertoire. If a preacher preached a sermon series on David one year, when Year B comes around again he or she could either read and preach on 1 and 2 Samuel texts that are excluded from the lectionary or read and preach on Chronicles or Ezra-Nehemiah. The guiding principle should be the same as that which structures Ordinary Time—not to jump from text to text but to provide enough of a particular body of literature that the congregation can begin to get a sense of its theological voice and perspective.

Since the lessons in Ordinary Time lend themselves so naturally to sermon series, the preacher does not need to leave the lectionary if he or she wants to preach a series. If, however, the preacher wants to preach a series that is more thematically than textually based, he or she can still be guided by the goals of Ordinary Time in selecting texts for such a series. Ordinary Time marks the regular progression of weeks, punctuated by the celebration of the Lord's Day. A thematic sermon series that honors that regular progression of time and text could still honor the possibilities of Ordinary Time while working with a slightly different textual repertoire.

Certain underrepresented biblical books can carry great power in the contemporary situation and so pastoral attention to the needs of a congregation can suggest ways to broaden a community's biblical repertoire. The Wisdom texts, which struggle with the perennial questions of the meaning of life and death, can model for contemporary Christians a way to think and talk about life and faith that does not trade merely in extremes and absolutes and does not settle for easy answers. The prophets asked their communities to struggle with questions of wealth and power. Were many of the difficult texts that the lectionary omits, both in the OT and the NT, restored to the worship life of contemporary communities, new ways to think about violence, judgment, and the shape of the future might become possible. The essential abandonment of Revelation by the lectionary, for example, has contributed to the sustained misunderstanding and misuse of this important book because many churches simply do not see modeled how it could be a regular part of the life of faith.

The decision when to vary from the lessons that are provided in the RCL also depends on the experience and length of ministry of the individual preacher. For the beginning preacher, who is working through the three-year lectionary cycle for the first time, the lessons available in Ordinary Time in the RCL provide more than sufficient material and grounding for the development of a preaching ministry and homiletical voice. The more experienced preacher, who has preached several rounds of the three-year cycle, will begin to notice what theological voices and perspectives are not represented in the lectionary and may want to address those limitations through alternate text selection.

NOTES

Preface

1. Even so, a few books, usually known to Protestants as the Apocrypha, are in dispute because Roman Catholics, Eastern Orthodox, and Anglicans include them, whereas, as a rule, Protestants tend to exclude them.

Chapter 1: An Introduction to Christian Lectionaries

1. This method of continuous reading is called *lectio continua*, about which there will be more in the next chapter.

2. Circumcision, that essential and unique mark of a male Jew, was traditionally done at home. It was not until medieval times in Europe that the *bris* was moved to the synagogue.

3. For a full treatment of the *Chaburah* meal, cf. Gregory Dix, *The Shape of the Liturgy*, (London: Dacre, 1956).

4. In late antiquity, the civilized way to drink wine was to mix it with water. It was thought that those who drank wine unmixed were drinking to get drunk. Drunkenness was one of the many false charges sometime leveled at "Christians."

5. Justin Martyr, *Apol.* 65-67.

6. J. A. Jungmann, *The Mass of the Roman Rite*, Vol. I (New York: Benziger, 1950), 398.

7. This custom is attested to in the Third Council of Carthage in 397 and although this is a post-Constantinian council it seems to assume a long tradition.

8. G. G. Willis, "St. Augustine's Lectionary" in *The Anglican Catholic* 44, 1962.

9. The Roman system of reading two Eucharistic lessons on a one-year cycle involved a one-year cycle of collects at the beginning of Mass. These set prayers usually picked up a theme from the church season or from the Gospel for the day. This reinforced the sense that each Sunday had its invariable themes such as "Good Shepherd Sunday," the Second Sunday in Easter, in which John 10:11-19 ("I am the good shepherd . . .") was paired with 1 Peter 2:19-25, in which Jesus' sacrifice is given as an example for Christians to follow and ends with the metaphor: "For you were going astray like sheep, but now you have returned to the shepherd and guardian of your souls."

The Collect Easter 2 picked up the themes of the Epistle, beginning: "Almighty God, you have given your only Son to be for us both a sacrifice for sin and an example of godly life." The introduction of a three-year lectionary means that the collects, which are still in weekly use in the Roman Catholic, Lutheran, and Anglican Churches, are no longer thematically related to the readings except in those nodal points in the church year, such as Christmas and Easter, where traditional readings have been retained. At this writing, some initial efforts to provide a coordinated three-year cycle of collects are being undertaken.

10. Cf. Paul F. Bradshaw, *Daily Prayer in the Early Church* (New York: Oxford University Press, 1982) and *The Search for the Origins of Christian Worship* (New York: Oxford University Press, 1992); Robert Taft, *The Liturgy of the Hours in East and West* (Collegeville, Minn.: Liturgical Press, 1993); J. G. Cumming, et al., "The Divine Office" in Jones, Cheslyn, et al., *The Study of Liturgy* (New York: Oxford University Press, 1978); and Paul Bradshaw, et al., "Daily Prayer" in Paul Bradshaw, ed., *The New Westminster Dictionary of Liturgy and Worship* (Louisville: Westminster John Knox Press, 2002). More recently there has been an interest in reviving the cathedral offices, especially in the Lutheran and Anglican traditions. This has raised the old problem of how to conjoin daily, systematic scripture reading with the church year.

11. *Ordo Romano* I, 64.

12. Thus the sermons of Leo I ("The Great"), Pope 440–461, almost always mark the time of the church year as it is being observed in the liturgy, refer to the appointed lessons for the day, and very often relate these in turn to the doctrine of the Incarnation, which he is at pains to explicate in terms of the Chalcedonian doctrine of the hypostatic union of the human and divine natures in one person.

13. At the same time, one must note that these designations remained different in different locations. Lessons followed local tradition and no one made a serious effort to standardize them in the West until the Carolingian period, and these efforts were not successful until the Council of Trent, by which time, of course, the Protestant churches had made their own several provisions for the manner of reading scripture.

14. Cf. Hippolytus, *The Apostolic Tradition*.

15. Although it took two hundred years and tragic losses such as that of the Nestorian Church in what is now Iraq, doctrinal unity was finally attained. Liturgy, however, remained a mix of local custom, regional use, and universal observance. Hence "families" of liturgies developed, such as the "Roman," the "Gallican," the "West Syrian," and the "Byzantine."

16. Chief among such offenses was apostasy. Not making a good confession when the authorities demanded a sacrifice of incense to the emperor's genius constituted the "unforgivable sin" against the Holy Spirit of Luke 12:10-12. However, mass persecutions such as those of Decian in 250–251 produced pastoral concerns such that by the later third century St. Cyprian of Carthage and others were developing procedures through which the "lapsed" might, after suitable repentance and penance, be reconciled and readmitted to Communion. This process of "canonical penance" as it came to be called, however, was long, arduous, and by no means automatic. It sought to honor the reality of Christian love and forgiveness while maintaining the strict purity of the church.

Chapter 2: The Church Year: The Christian's History

1. Nevertheless, pilgrimages formed a very important part of medieval life. Many actually did go to the Holy Land, and many more who did not have the means to undertake this long and arduous trip contented themselves with pilgrimages to more proximate holy sites such as Walsingham or Canterbury in England. The former is particularly interesting because its attraction was an eleventh century "replica" of the house in which Jesus lived with Mary and Joseph in Nazareth. The latter was the site of the martyrdom of Thomas A. Becket.

2. The celebration of Easter on Sunday was a matter of controversy until the fifth century. Jesus' actual resurrection is reported in the Gospels as having been on "the first day of the week," which is to say on Sunday, nicely making it the first day of the "New Creation," just as the first creation in Genesis began on Sunday. However, since the first Easter was related to Passover, making the original Exodus a "type" of Jesus "passing over" from death to life and so saving Christians from bondage to sin and death, many early

Christian communities calculated Easter by the Jewish reckoning of Passover, that is, on the fourteenth of Nisan. Of course, this custom meant that Easter was usually celebrated on a day other than Sunday. A group of churches in Asia, centered in Ephesus, were so wedded to this "Quartodeciman" practice that they maintained themselves as a separate sect until the fifth century.

3. From very early on, Christians had adapted the Jewish custom of fasting twice a week but chose Wednesdays and Fridays instead of Mondays and Thursdays to distinguish themselves from Judaism.

4. Cf. Council of Nicaea, Canon 5.

5. Cf. Thomas J. Talley, *The Origins of the Christian Year*, 2nd ed. (Collegeville, Minn.: Liturgical Press, 1991).

6. From the sixth century, the calendar contained a three-week preparation for Lent. These Sundays were called *Septuagesima*, *Sexigesima*, and *Quinquagesima*. *Quinquagesima* Sunday marked fifty days before Easter, whereas the other two, counting backwards, yielded inaccurate approximations of sixty and seventy days before Easter. In the West the readings for *Septuagesima* Sunday became associated with Creation. In the East the readings addressed the themes of judgment and forgiveness. At the Reformation, those churches that retained the liturgical year continued the pre-lenten season. The consensus of the twentieth-century liturgical movement was that a season of preparation for a season of preparation was redundant and confusing and so the "gesima" Sundays were eliminated. This allowed for the insertion of the Transfiguration as the Gospel for the last Sunday of Epiphany, making a dramatic climax for the season of Christ's manifestation and providing a marked contrast to the theme of humility in Lent.

7. The nomenclature "Ordinary Time" is a product of the twentieth-century liturgical movement. Formerly, this was understood broadly as the season of the Holy Spirit and the unfolding of Scripture in terms of its existential meaning for each person was part of the work of the Spirit. Some medieval rites used red as the liturgical color throughout this season in order to make this point. After the fourteenth-century adaptation of the Feast of the Holy Trinity on the Sunday following Pentecost, some churches began counting "Sundays after Trinity." Sarum adopted this custom, and so it passed, until recently, into subsequent editions of *The Book of Common Prayer*. For years The United Methodist Church, following the impetus of the nineteenth-century theological emphasis on "building the kingdom of God on earth," designated this time as "Kingdomtide."

8. Peter G. Cobb, "The History of the Christian Year" in Chesslyn Jones, et al., *The Study of Liturgy* (New York: Oxford University Press, 1978), 416.

9. Clement of Alexandria, *Stromateis*, VII, 6. This notion, like most early references to post-mortem purification by fire, is based on the famously difficult passage in 1 Corinthians 3:11-15.

10. See, for instance, the narrative of the passion and death of St. Perpetua, which is attributed with probability to Tertullian. In that account, dating from perhaps the early third century, the saint, incarcerated and waiting for her death in the arena, is visited with a dream about her brother Dinocratus, who had died some years earlier with a disfiguring cancer. She sees the lad, disfigured, dirty, and unhappy, trying to get a drink of water from a bowl he cannot reach. She awakens saddened and prays for him daily. Soon she has another dream in which little Dinocratus is healed, clean, and happy in some sort of lovely playground, drinking deeply from a golden bowl of water.

Chapter 3: The Lectionary as Hermeneutic

1. The *kerygma* of the early church included the injunction to "repent and be baptized." Paul (Rom 2:4-5) certainly sees repentance as necessary and, in fact, as the goal of God's

kindness and patience with us. Thus one must ask the extent to which contrition, an affective category, is necessarily connected to *metanoia*, or changing one's mind-set.

2. Note that the third set of lessons for Christmas Eve and Day, as well as the First Sunday after Christmas, is the Prologue to John, traditionally the preeminent text of the doctrine of the Incarnation as opposed to the birth of Jesus.

Chapter 4: Preaching the Lectionary Today

1. A helpful discussion of the different perspectives of Catholic and Protestant approaches to the place of the lectionary in corporate worship appears in the first three chapters of Fritz West, *Scripture and Memory: The Ecumenical Hermeneutic of the Three-Year Lectionaries* (Collegeville, Minn.: Liturgical Press, 1997).

2. The RCL contains an interesting concession to the January 1/December 31 cycle by providing readings for January 1.

3. For a more detailed discussion of the history of the development of Ordinary Time, see chapter 2; for a more detailed discussion of preaching in Ordinary Time, see chapter 7.

4. Other lectionary cycles establish the interrelationship of the Sundays of Ordinary Time by identifying them according to consecutive numbers. The lectionary of the Episcopal Church, found in the *Book of Common Prayer*, refers to the Sundays of Ordinary Time as "Propers" and assigns each Proper a number (for example, Proper 19, Proper 20, Proper 21).

5. For a very accessible history of the development of the lectionaries through the 1970s, see John Reumann, "A History of Lectionaries: From the Synagogue at Nazareth to Post–Vatican II," *Interpretation* 31 (1977): 116-30.

6. For a history of the Consultation on Common Texts (CCT), consult the CCT website, http://commontexts.org.

7. For a discussion of the issues that shaped the final form of the RCL, see the introduction.

8. For a list of the countries and churches or ecclesiastical communities that use the RCL, see "Worldwide Usage of the *Revised Common Lectionary*," www.commontexts.org.

Chapter 5: Preaching the Incarnational Cycle

1. In some places the third of the four candles on the "Advent Wreath" is rose-colored. In some places on this Sunday, the vestments and other hangings are also rose. This follows the medieval custom of observing "Gaudete" (L. *gaudere* meaning "to rejoice") Sunday so named because of the Introit (or Entrance Song) for this day: "Rejoice in the Lord always; and again I will say, Rejoice" (Phil 4:4). Gaudete Sunday became customary as a mirror of "Laetare" (L. *Laetari* meaning "rejoice") Sunday from the Introit: "Rejoice with Jerusalem, and be glad for her" (Isa 66:10a). Laetare is the Fourth Sunday in Lent ("Mid-Lent") in which the extremely arduous fasting regimen of monasteries might be relaxed somewhat. So this was also called "Refreshment Sunday," and the violet-colored vestments were lightened somewhat, eventually becoming rose-colored by consensus.

2. The recent recovery of the centrality of the Pasch and the primary importance of the *triduum* as the mother of all Christian celebrations simply has not reached many Christians and, as fraught with the dangers of sentimentality as it may be, Christmas Eve remains the most real "touchstone" in the Christian year for many. The dangers of sentimentality can be best addressed by reference to both the implications of the Incarnation for the redemption of human nature and creation and the social implications of the coming of Messiah.

3. So important is the existential situation of the reader in her or his social and personal location at the time of reading that this exercise of reading and charting should be redone every year. For example, Charles Hackett has seen Arthur Miller's great play *The Death of a Salesman* three times. The first time, in my late adolescence, it seemed to me to be a clear indictment of capitalism and its destructive powers of alienation. When I saw it again in my thirties, it appeared as a tragic accounting of the human situation so well described by Sartre and other "existentialists." The last time I saw it, in the late 1970s, it now appeared as a painful delineation of the working out of a narcissistic personality disorder. Even leaving room for the interpretations of three different casts, it seems to me evident that these three quite different takes on the play were largely the result of the hermeneutical lenses I brought to it at different times in my life. At the same time, one must also say that the play does "carry" these three senses. Of course, it is a tribute to Miller's genius that his play can so carry in itself these three and no doubt many other serious interpretations. If this is true of an Arthur Miller play, how much more true of Scripture!

Chapter 6: Preaching the Easter (Paschal) Cycle

1. One should note that the *manner* of this presence as implied in Jesus' words depends on church tradition. Thus, Roman Catholic, Anglican, and Lutheran hearers would tend to identify that presence as "in" the bread in some way, whereas others might be inclined to hear it metaphorically as a reminder of Jesus' presence in one's heart.

2. Hoyt L. Hickman, et al., ed., *The New Handbook of the Christian Year* (Nashville: Abingdon Press, 1992).

3. The exegetical awkwardness that this division creates is an important first impression. It is an important reminder that all biblical passages in the lectionary are but a small sampling of the larger biblical text from which they come. All the lessons for Ash Wednesday are pieces of larger texts (none of the Ash Wednesday lessons provides a continuous reading through a passage), selected to highlight themes that are central to the Ash Wednesday context in particular and the paschal cycle more broadly.

4. In order to make clear that the Sixth Sunday in Lent consists of two sets of readings (one for the liturgy of the palms and one for the liturgy of the Passion), the charting for this Sunday is presented on a separate table.

Chapter 7: Preaching in Ordinary Time

1. Because the date of Easter can shift dramatically, depending on the coordination of the lunar calendar and the spring equinox, the distribution of Sundays in Ordinary Time varies from year to year. When Easter is late—and hence Ash Wednesday is late—there are more Sundays between Epiphany and Lent than there are in years when Ash Wednesday is early. That is why there is such variation in the numbering of Sundays in Ordinary Time. The spread of calendar days that are included in the RCL listings after Pentecost (for example, Sunday between September 25 and October 1 inclusive) provides a way to count the Sundays that takes into account the variations in the dates of Lent and Easter. Some traditions refer to these numbered Sundays as "propers." This terminology is also reflected in the listings in the RCL.

2. Hickman, *The New Handbook of the Christian Year*, 33.

3. As, for example, in the following quote from Chrysostom, Homily 7, John 1:9:

> The reason, O children greatly beloved, why we entertain you portion by portion with the thoughts taken from the Scriptures, and do not at once pour all forth to you, is, that the retaining what is successively set before you may be easy. For even in building, one who before the first stones are settled lays on others, constructs a rotten wall altogether, and easily thrown

down while one who waits that the mortar may first get hard, and so adds what remains little by little, finishes the whole house firmly, and makes it strong, not one to last for a short time, or easily to fall to pieces. These builders we imitate, and in like manner build up your souls. For we fear lest, while the first foundation is but newly laid, the addition of the succeeding speculations may do harm to the former, through the insufficiency of the intellect to contain them all at once.

What now is it that has been read to us today?

4. For a discussion of this by the Consultation of Common Texts, the ecumenical committee responsible for the RCL, see "Frequently asked questions about the *Revised Common Lectionary*," http://www.commontexts.org/rcl/faq.html.

5. For a discussion of the importance of moving away from the typological approach to the Hebrew Scriptures in the Roman Catholic *Lectionary for Mass*, see Gerard S. Sloyan, "Some Suggestions for a Biblical Three-Year Lectionary," *Worship* 63.6 (1989): 521-35.

6. See the "Introduction," *The Revised Common Lectionary*, *The Consultation on Common Texts* (Nashville: Abingdon Press, 1992), 14-19.

7. As noted in chapter 5, the final Sundays after Pentecost focus on eschatological themes and on the Reign of Christ, as the year begins to make the turn toward Advent. On those Sundays, the selection of the first lesson is determined by the Gospel lesson for the day.

8. See Fritz West, *Scripture and Memory* (Collegeville, Minn.: Liturgical Press, 1997) and "Scripture, Bible, and Lectionary: A Quest for Common Ground," *Worship* 74 (2000): 290-307.

9. For the discussion and examples that follow, "Ordinary Time" is shorthand for "Sundays after Pentecost."

10. The RCL often provides some verses in parentheses. These verses normally fill out the context of the lesson. They are in parentheses to indicate that the preacher can choose whether to read the longer version of the passage in worship.

11. This phrase comes from Gerard S. Sloyan, "The Lectionary as a Context for Interpretation," *Interpretation* 31 (1977): 131-38.

12. In this chapter, we are not including discussion of the psalm that is appointed for each day. The psalm can be used a preaching text, but more often the psalm is used in worship as a congregational response to the other lessons. The psalms follow a pattern of selected reading, not continuous, as they are selected to reflect the theme of one of the lessons, usually either the other OT lesson or the Gospel.

13. In fact, for the Gospel lessons, the preacher could begin the mapping exercise after Epiphany if he or she chose. As we have noted, for the Sundays between Epiphany and Lent, the first and second lessons (OT and Epistle) are selected in relationship to the Gospel lesson and so are not part of the mapping proposed here. For those Sundays, the most effective strategy is simply to look a Sunday at a time.

14. Depending on when Lent begins in a given year, any of the following Sundays (six through nine, or propers 1-4) could be the Last Sunday before Ash Wednesday. In some traditions, the Last Sunday after the Epiphany is observed as Transfiguration Sunday, and the Gospel lesson in Year B for that Sunday is Mark 9:2-9. In other traditions, the story of the Transfiguration is the Gospel lesson for the Second Sunday in Lent. In addition, when the Sundays after Epiphany are shortened by the beginning of Lent, the lessons that would have been read on those Sundays are simply dropped for that year. The congregation then hears less of the opening chapters of the year's Gospel.

15. Although technically a Sunday in Ordinary Time, Trinity Sunday is its own liturgical feast in the calendar and so has lessons selected for that day. It does not employ semicontinuous reading for any of the lessons.

16. Depending on the timing of Lent and Easter, the semi-continuous reading of the Gospel could resume with the lesson for the Eighth Sunday (see previous chart). This was discussed earlier in the chapter. The Mark 2:23–3:6 reading here assumes that the Transfiguration story was read on the last Sunday before Ash Wednesday.

17. In Ordinary Time, the RCL listing of lessons provides two options for the first lesson. The first option is the semi-continuous reading, which is the reading that will be mapped here. The second option follows the Roman Catholic pattern of selected reading and provides an OT lesson that is selected because of its thematic connection to the Gospel lesson. Because the pattern of semi-continuous reading of the OT is the signal contribution and innovation of the RCL, we will only attend to those lessons in this chapter.

18. Interestingly, Hannah's song is used instead of a Psalm reading for the Thirty-third Sunday after Pentecost in this cycle in order to complement the other lessons for that day but is not part of the continuous reading of the books of Samuel.

19. Readings from 2 Corinthians start with the Seventh Sunday after the Epiphany. Those readings are Seventh Sunday, 2 Corinthians 1:18-22; Eighth Sunday, 2 Corinthians 3:1-6.

20. Cf. the omission of texts of violence and judgment from the David narrative.

21. Hickman, *The New Handbook of the Christian Year,* 242.

22. See Wade P. Huie, Jr., "Lectionaries Offer Freedom," *Reformed Liturgy and Music* 24 (1990): 183-186. Quoting from this article, Fritz West ("Scripture, Bible, and Lectionary," p. 291) notes Huie's analysis of a survey of eight years of one preacher's sermons: no sermons on nineteen books of the Bible, only one sermon from eighteen other books, and less than 20% of the total sermons on OT texts.

23. As cited in Hans Walter Wolff, *Old Testament and Christian Preaching* (Philadelphia: Fortress Press, 1986). See also, " 'I believe; help my unbelief': Bonhoeffer on Biblical Preaching," *Word and World* 26/1 (2006): 86-97.

24. See, for example, Nancy Lammers Gross, *If You Cannot Preach Like Paul . . .* (Grand Rapids, Mich.: Eerdmans, 2002) and Brad R. Braxton, *Preaching Paul* (Nashville: Abingdon Press, 2004).